D1250333

PERSEVERING POPULIST

THE LIFE OF FRANK DOSTER

KF
3 73
. D6
B7

PERSEVERING POPULIST

THE LIFE OF
FRANK DOSTER

BY MICHAEL J. BRODHEAD

UNIVERSITY OF NEVADA PRESS
RENO, NEVADA
1969

WITHDRAWN

THE LIBRARY
INDIANA STATE UNIVERSITY
EVANSVILLE CAMPUS

065428

UNIVERSITY OF NEVADA PRESS
RENO, NEVADA

© 1969 by University of Nevada Press
Library of Congress Catalog Card Number 69-20037

DESIGNED BY KEN WEBSTER
PRINTED IN THE UNITED STATES OF AMERICA

SBN 87417-024-9

TO JAMES C. MALIN

In the current debates over the nature of the Populist movement, the disputants have stressed the need for local and biographical studies. With the possible exception of Annie L. Diggs's eulogistic life of Jerry Simpson, there are no full length biographies of any of the leaders of Kansas Populism. The present study, an account of the career of Frank Doster, attempts to fill gaps in both the biography and the local history of the movement.

Doster was a Virginia-born, Indiana-raised Kansas lawyer who rose from a district judgeship to become Chief Justice of the Kansas Supreme Court from 1897 to 1903. His tenure in public office alone justifies some attention to his life and work. More importantly, his contemporaries, both friendly and hostile, considered him to be one of the leading expositors of reform ideas during the Populist period. As a disseminator of reform ideology, moreover, he was a significant figure long before and long after the short life of Populism. His adult career began during the Civil War and ended a few days before the launching of the New Deal; he was associated with the Republican, Greenback, Union Labor, People's, and Democratic parties at various points in his life. Often he referred to himself as a socialist, and shortly before his death he defended the communist experiment in the Soviet Union.

Frank Doster was but one of several talented and articulate men in Kansas who popularized proposals for change during the late nineteenth and early twentieth centuries. For most of that period people like him—lawyers, ministers, editors, and businessmen of all political faiths—provided intellectual leadership in the state. In this respect they were collectively more important than the state's universities and colleges. Through their editorials, speeches, novels, articles, sermons, and poems, their thoughts reached the smallest villages and most isolated farms. Although their ideas were not necessarily original or brilliant, many of these men attained a degree of sophistication and erudition which may surprise the reader of today.

The superficial accounts of the Populist crusade, which emphasized its colorful leaders, ignored Doster. He had no flowing beard; he was never known to want for socks; and he was not a woman. Recent scholarly studies have paid attention to his role and have done much to place him in the proper perspective; but the author has had all the joy of examining the life of this singular, complex man for the first time in detail. He "discovered" the subject of this work while researching his master's thesis on E. W. Hoch, governor of Kansas from 1905 to 1909. Upon beginning the research he had never heard of Hoch's fellow townsman, Frank Doster, even though he grew up in the community in which both men began their careers. Soon, however, Doster's importance to the Populist and related movements became evident.

Some will wonder why the writer has not related his findings to the questions raised about Populism in the latest interpretations of the movement. The answer is simply that these questions were not important to Doster and his colleagues. Today's debates about the agrarian protest of the late nineteenth century relate largely to present problems and ideologies. The major consideration in current arguments is whether Populism belongs in the mainstream of modern liberalism. The writer is hidebound enough to believe that such concerns are not the province of the historian or biographer. Even if they were, too little is known about Populism and the people in it to give definitive answers.

Like so many Kansas Populists, Doster left little in the way of correspondence and other manuscripts. It was necessary to reconstruct his life largely from contemporary newspapers and public documents. In doing so, the staff of the Kansas State Historical Society rendered invaluable aid. Chief among those who made working there thoroughly enjoyable were Robert W. Richmond, Joseph W. Snell, Eugene Decker, Thomas Grogg, Lela Barnes, Forrest Blackburn, Elsie Beine, and Alberta Pantle. All but one of the illustrations herein appear through the courtesy of the Kansas State Historical Society, Topeka.

Residents of Marion were able to give useful information and suggestions. David and D. W. Wheeler, Wharton Hoch, Alex Case, and Mrs. Helen Goodsheller were particularly helpful. John and Mildred Riddle of Salina provided much of the data on John's uncle Frank Doster's last days. Special thanks are due to Caroline Doster Price who kindly allowed the author to examine and reproduce the manuscripts of her grandfather's speeches.

Three graduate students working on related topics have my thanks for sharing their knowledge and for directing me to sources which otherwise would have been overlooked: Sister M. Berard McKenna of St. Louis University, and Orval Clanton and Robert La Forte of the University of Kansas. They also served who sat and listened patiently while the author thought out loud; and my friends Lee M. Peters, John G. Gagliardo, Robert E. Bonner, Donald B. Unger, Charles R. Bowlus, and

Arly H. Allen performed valiant service. Professors Paul E. Wilson and C. D. Clark of the University of Kansas offered valuable information. Miss Laura Neiswanger gave the manuscript a thorough reading and, in her sweet way, pointed out numerous errors. The insights and factual data given by James C. Malin were indispensable.

Professors Rodney C. Loehr and W. Donald Beatty of the University of Minnesota read the manuscript and offered helpful suggestions. Colleagues at the University of Nevada— James W. Hulse, Harold L. Kirkpatrick, George Herman, Elmer R. Rusco, and Robert P. Laxalt—supplied corrections and encouragement. This study was prepared originally as a dissertation under Clarke A. Chambers of the University of Minnesota. No one could ask for a more considerate and helpful advisor.

Reno, Nevada   M.J.B.
November, 1968

CONTENTS

1

ONCE A VERY POPULAR MAN
IN MARION COUNTY

L IKE MANY LEADERS of the agrarian uprising of the 1890's,
Frank Doster was a professional man and a town-
dweller rather than a farmer. His antecedents and up-
bringing, however, were wholly agricultural and rural. The
Doster family was established in America in 1717 when a
Würtemburg peasant, Thomas Doster, emigrated from Germany. His grandson Alfred inherited the family farm located
in Morgan County, Virginia. To Alfred and his wife Rachel
Doyle were born three sons. Frank, the youngest, was born
on January 19, 1847, near the town of Winchester.

The following year Alfred Doster took his family to Indiana,
settling on a Clinton County farm. There is little information
on the youngest Doster's childhood and immediate family environment. Whether his Hoosier parents were poor or com-
fortably fixed is not known. As in all personal matters, Doster
was closemouthed about his early life and parentage. In an age
much given to tracing of ancestry and personal reminiscences,
it is strange to find one so reluctant to tell others of his antecedents and youth; yet it is typical of the man. His private and
public lives were strictly separated. History is robbed of any
clues as to early influences on his radicalism. Whether it was
poverty, dislike of parental authority, the romantic idealism

of the era, or the existence of objective grievances, we cannot know; and the record is too scanty to invite speculation.[1]

The coming of the Civil War presented an opportunity for a grand adventure to the farm boy. As he admitted in his last years, his eagerness to serve stemmed not from patriotism, but from a lust for excitement and drama. It is said that at the age of fourteen he ran away to aid the militia in driving Morgan's raiders out of Indiana. In his pension application of January, 1915, he notes that he served with "Co. G. 105 Ind. State Legion."[2]

Then the young militiaman returned to the farm; in the meantime his two elder brothers had joined the Union forces. By 1864 both were dead, one of wounds received near Mill Springs, Kentucky, the other of smallpox. Thus Frank was the only surviving son of Alfred and Rachel Doster. The death of his brothers, however, did not dampen his military ardor. On January 30, 1864, at Delphi, Indiana, he enlisted as a private in Company M of the Eleventh Indiana Cavalry. Although he was barely seventeen, he gave his age as eighteen. In his pension application he admitted that his age on his enlistment papers "was probably overstated for fear of being rejected if correctly stated." To make doubly sure of acceptance, he enlisted under his father's name. For his enlistment for a three-year period, he was entitled to a bounty totaling three hundred dollars. The regimental records describe him as being five feet six inches in height, with a fair complexion, light hair, and grey eyes.[3]

His brigade was sent immediately to the South—first to Tennessee and then to Mississippi. Shortly after its arrival in Mississippi, the war ended. Instead of being discharged, the men of the Eleventh were ordered to ride to Kansas for use as escort parties along the Santa Fe Trail. Years later Doster recalled the entry of his unit into the West: "Newly mounted and armed at St. Louis, we rode through the Ozark hills of Missouri, through Rolla, Sedalia and smaller towns, crossing the line into Kansas at the now unknown hamlet of Little Santa Fe."[4]

From there they passed to Olathe and Lawrence. At Lawrence the local newspaper described the Eleventh Indiana as a "fine body of men, somewhat tattered and worn by long marches and by the smoke of hard-fought battles, and as they marched through our streets led by their gallant colonel Sharra, presented an imposing appearance. This regiment was with General Wilson before Nashville, and thence through the southern confederacy, and has made a fine record." From Lawrence they passed through Topeka, Fort Riley, and Council Grove—"then," Doster wrote, "the jumping-off place of civilization." Beyond Council Grove was "the great mysterious land of legend and adventure."[5]

Doster recollected in later years that his comrades knew nothing of their mission. Some supposed that they were being sent to Mexico to expel the Emperor Maximilian. Others believed they were on the plains to quell an Indian uprising, for there were stories of dreadful depredations on the border. The record shows, however, that the Indians were relatively peaceful in that period. Doster's own suspicion was that "our business was to take part in what the military strategists call 'a demonstration in force'—an armed parade to impress the Indian with the fact that he 'was up agin it.' He had been troublesome during the war, and there being now troops to spare, the design was to scare him—lick him, if need be—into good behavior."[6]

His regiment moved on into the then unsettled central portion of Kansas. Most of his company remained at Moore's

ranch, a way-station on the Santa Fe Trail in Marion County
—Doster's future home. But Doster accompanied the main
body of the regiment further south and west to Forts Zarah,
Larned, and Dodge. He later worte that they had probably
been employed as dispatch bearers. Traveling "at courier
speed" they reached Lyons, then turned eastward to rejoin
their respective companies.

As an old man it seemed to him that "the greatest excursion
that could then be taken by a tough, healthy boy was a
summer's horseback ride out of the Santa Fe Trail on the
Arkansas."

> Blazing hot it was, dusty from the tramp of innumerable
> hoofs and rolling of many wheels; but on each side [of] the
> worn track of travel were the freedom of the unfenced green-
> sward and the stretches of limitless distance. There too was
> restful sleep with the bare grass for a couch and the stars for
> covering, the opal and crimson sunrise of morning, the shim-
> mering heat of day with its curious and deceptive mirage,
> the gorgeous sunsets of red and gold, seen only on the open
> plains and the open sea, followed again by the untroubled
> oblivion of night. Then too, there was the dramatic sense of
> adventure, pleasing to a boy of ardent disposition—a sort of
> fanciful make-believe challenge to the fates that might be
> lurking just out of sight on the near-by stretches of the
> plains.[7]

After rejoining his company, Doster was detailed—much to
his dismay—to make a two-day ride to the south with an escort party. At the time he did not know the purpose of the
expedition. Later he learned that they were escorting General
John R. Sanborn to the junction of the Big and Little Arkansas rivers. There Sanborn was to make the preliminary negotiations for a treaty between the United States and the Kiowas,
Comanches, Arapahoes, and Apaches, by which the Indians
were to abandon the region between the Platte and the Ar-

kansas rivers. Knowing nothing of what was happening, the youthful cavalryman (by then a corporal) "laid on the grass under the shade of the cottonwoods and fought flies and cussed the powwow for not hurrying through to an end." In his reminiscences, Doster offered an explanation for his indifference:

> I was a boy, scant eighteen years old. I had been away from home more than a year and a half. The war was over and I wanted to return. But a short while back I had been where the drama of the great events was played. I had seen the blossoming of flags of ten thousand on parade and had heard the 'shoutings of the captain.' A convocation of filthy Indian bucks grunting a jargon I could not understand about something I did not know, consuming the time I wanted to put in going home, was not of a nature to excite my interested attention. It had in it neither the thrill of adventure nor the charm of sight-seeing.[8]

When the mission of the Eleventh Indiana Cavalry in the West was accomplished, the regiment was ordered back for discharge. On September 19, 1865, Corporal Doster, along with the other members of Company M, was mustered out at Fort Leavenworth, Kansas. He gladly returned to his home and family; yet he counted his months of service as beneficial. Army life had indeed been important for him. In the first place it allowed him to take a close look at the area in which he would settle and begin a career. His widow's recollections state that while in Marion County he had asked local promoter Levi Billings about prospects for a young attorney in the raw frontier area and Billings had encouraged him to return. Also, his army experience made him an unabashed militarist for the greater part of his life.[9]

Back in Indiana, Doster entered Thornton Academy. There one of his instructors was John Clark Ridpath, later a writer of popular histories and a supporter of radical causes. The young veteran next enrolled in the state university and later studied at Benton Law Institute. Apparently he never completed his formal training at either institution, for he received no degrees after four years of course work. Instead, he moved to Monticello, Illinois, where, on July 29, 1870, he married Caroline Riddle. His wife was a talented girl, well educated by the standards of the day, having attended the Jacksonville Female Academy. The young couple spent the first months of married life in the home of her parents where young Frank occupied his days studying law.[10]

In 1870 Doster was admitted to the Illinois bar. He practiced briefly in Monticello, but was, according to Caroline Doster's statement, committed to the plan of settling in Marion Centre, the prairie community in south central Kansas which had struck him as a good place for a young professional man. His father-in-law, an old frontiersman, forbade them to make the trip in the winter. "Carrie" recollected that she sewed, painted, and made rag rugs and baby clothes (for she was then pregnant) while they waited for the spring.

Finally, in March of 1871, Frank set out alone for the new country in order to make the initial preparations. According to his wife, he rode by train to Cottonwood Falls, Kansas; from there he journeyed by stage to Council Grove and walked the remaining miles to his destination. Subsisting on the remnant of food prepared for the railroad journey and spending the night at a "terrible hovel," he arrived in Marion Centre the following evening.

Carrie was soon able to join her husband. Traveling by train, she arrived at Cottonwood Falls. There she found Frank waiting—"so burned and brown from the wind that he was almost unrecognizable." Together they travelled by stage to Marion County, some thirty miles distant.

Well might the young couple have had misgivings about their new home. Marion County, lying on the edge of settlement in Kansas, had a population of about eight hundred. The town of Marion Centre, although the county seat, had only two hundred residents and no railroad. Doster's wife remembered Marion Centre as a village of one street fifteen-hundred feet long which ran at a right angle to the stream passing through the town. Among the businesses in operation at the time of the Dosters' arrival were three general stores, two land offices, a drug store, newspaper, butcher shop, livery stable, and hotel. Carrie Doster recalled that they were unable to spend their first nights in the hotel, since they would have been required to share a loft with rough Texas cowboys. So the couple lived for about ten days in a lean-to attached to a cabin, eating an unvaried diet of rice, potatoes, poor quality side meat, and dried apples.[11]

The prospects in other parts of the county were also none too pleasing to recent immigrants from the East; situated on the western edge of the Flint Hills, the entire county was described by the Kansas State Board of Agriculture as 98 percent prairie. It was the period before the fertility of the semiarid regions was generally recognized. Another two decades would pass before settlers realized that wheat and not corn was the most suitable crop for the region.

The area could have been more appealing had the frontier myth been applicable there, but, as with most of the trans-Mississippi West, it was not. The Santa Fe Railway corporation owned 97,716 of the best acres of Marion County land. It was then being sold through the local firm of Case and Billings at prices from $3.50 to $9.00 an acre. Even if a settler could obtain a free quarter-section homestead or purchase one by preemption, the cost of breaking the sod was $3.00 an acre. Fencing was also expensive.[12]

Unpromising though it must have appeared, the Dosters remained. Carrie described their first substantial dwelling as a small, weather-boarded building of two rooms which had formerly been a harness shop. To furnish it, they bought a table, bedstead, kitchen stove, and a few chairs. From two packing boxes Doster fashioned a cupboard and a place for their clothing.

Carrie Doster also remembered some anxious moments arising from the presence of Indians. In time she became accustomed to them, for they frequently passed through Marion Centre on the way to their hunting grounds in Indian Territory. Carrie recalled that once her fear of them passed, she would invite them in for refreshments; she was amused by their fascination with the glitter of her silver forks. Her only fear was that they would steal the "gay quilt" from the crib of their baby Lenore.[13]

Once settled, Frank Doster established his law practice. Speaking nearly forty years later, Congressman Samuel R. Peters, once a colleague of Doster's in the old Ninth Judicial District (Chase, Marion, and Butler counties and the unorganized counties of southwestern Kansas), described the lawyers of the district in the early 1870's: "The members of the Bar at that time were nearly all young men, comparatively new in the practice with scanty libraries. As a rule they were energetic, studious, ambitious and in most of the counties the only books of reference were a few standard works, together with the statutes and twelve Kansas reports."[14]

In the year of his arrival in Marion Centre, Doster went into a partnership with a notary public, one E. Baxter. In addition to its legal and notarial services, the firm of Baxter and Doster sold Santa Fe lands for three to ten dollars an acre on eleven years' time at 7 percent—a strange beginning for an agrarian reformer! Also the firm advertised for sale "a large and well-selected list of superior Farming Lands, Stock Farms, &c, &c, in Marion and adjoining counties belonging to individuals, ranging in price from two to ten dollars per acre." The "individuals" were eastern landholders who had engrossed so much Marion County land that local promoters announced that henceforth immigrants must buy from the absentee speculators or the Santa Fe. One firm announced that it owned 31,000 choice acres in the county.

Those wishing to take up government lands under the Preemption Act of 1841 and the Homestead Act of 1862 could secure them through Baxter and Doster "thus saving all the time and trouble, and almost all the entire expense of a trip to the U.S. Land Office." The partners performed still other services: "We draft Deeds, Mortgages, Title Bonds, Leases, Wills, Powers of Attorney, and Contracts." Another advertisement informed the public that "Frank Doster . . . Attorney at Law! Will practice in Southern Kansas and in the United States Land Office."

After a few months the partnership was dissolved. The local paper announced, on January 14, 1872, that a Mr. Rockafield had purchased Doster's interest in the land office.[15]

Even as the country was becoming more settled and tame, the practice of law still had its hazards. Doster's wife told of an incident in 1872 that was her "first real taste of the dangers besetting pioneers." Her husband, along with a client, had set out in a lumber wagon for Salina, some sixty miles distant. En route they were caught in a blizzard. Knowing that there were few homes along the way in which they could seek shelter, Carrie Doster lay awake all night, able to rest only after her husband returned safely.[16]

Like many a lawyer in the frontier environment, Doster was drawn to politics. As befitted a Union veteran in Kansas with political ambitions, he was a straight-out Republican. Politics in Kansas, as elsewhere in the nation, was particularly venal in the post-war period. The West, like the South, was a happy hunting ground for political adventurers. Kansas "carpetbaggers" such as the notorious Senator Samuel C. Pomeroy (Mark Twain's "Senator Dilworthy" of *The Gilded Age*) set the tone for governmental morality. In those days of chartering railroads, erecting capital buildings, and parceling out colleges and other state institutions to the various localities, jobbery was rife. There were many opportunities for place and pelf, and the Kansas politicos of the seventies were on hand to take them.

Before 1877, legislators were elected annually. Frequent elections gave rise to a corps of full-time politicians. After 1877 and the biennial election of legislators, the professional politicians were no longer necessary. As they died off or left the state, their places were filled by the young men of Doster's generation, with whom politics was more avocation than vocation.

In 1871, the residents of Marion County were interested in but one issue to be fought out in the Topeka cockpit during the next legislative session. The western counties, with few adequate materials for fence-building, suffered from the destruction of crops by the Texas cattle driven through their prairies. In time they would have a technological remedy—barbed wire; but in those years they sought a legislative solution—a "herd law" which would force the drovers to exercise greater control over their stock.[17]

The Republican county convention chose Doster as its nominee in October of 1871. Campaigning on a herd-law platform, the popular young attorney won easily. His opponent, R. C. Bates, running on a bolting "People's ticket," lost to the nominee of the regulars by a vote of 293 to 179.[18]

In January Doster went to Topeka to take his seat. At twenty-six he was the youngest member of the 1872 legislature. Despite his youth, he was placed on the powerful Committee on Agriculture and Manufacturing. More importantly for his purposes, he was one of fifteen members of a special committee to consider and report "all bills in reference to herd, hedge, stock and fence laws."[19]

As he had promised, Doster sent letters to the *Marion County Record* to keep his constituents abreast of legislative affairs. The political neophyte was shocked at some of the goings-on among his colleagues. Having supposed that "dignity always characterized the deliberations of a legislative body," he was struck by the lack of it in this session. "My ideal legislator having evaporated, may then be my excuse for turning critic." Yet, despite the "confusion and lack of order . . . incident to legislation," Doster noted that many constructive measures were receiving the attention they deserved; and "the shysters, whose legislative ability is exhausted in the 'ring' manipulations and wire pulling incident to the election of clerks and pages have now, like Othello, 'found their occupation gone,' and have given place to active and substantial workers."

In the same letter Doster was pleased to report that the herd-law question was the major issue before the legislators. "I am glad it is receiving that consideration which its importance demands. At least twenty bills have been introduced thus far relating to the subject, the provisions of every one of which contemplates the relief of the farmer from trespassing animals. A special committee, of which your humble servant is a member, has been selected to which all bills bearing on the subject are referred, and out of these I think we shall be able to dijest [sic] something of benefit and justice to all parties, and which the courts will also hold good."[20]

In his next letter to the Record, Doster first informed the readers of the pending investigation of corruption in the 1867 election of Senators Pomeroy and Caldwell. Turning to the matter closest to their hearts, Doster told his fellow citizens of the progress of the herd law. He was surprised to find that the lines being drawn for and against such legislation were not as sectional as had been supposed, for "many members from the eastern counties are favorable to the law, while some from the west oppose it."[21]

On the House floor, Doster fought hard for the desired law. He presented two petitions from Marion County residents asking for a herd law. The special committee of which he was a member received "not less than two dozen" bills on the subject, but the committee rejected them all and put forward its own substitute. There were doubts about the substitute's constitutionality, however, and Doster informed the citizens of his district of yet another bill to be introduced soon, "different from anything yet presented, which many friends of the measure approve as being better than the one reported by the committee."[22]

Perhaps Doster was referring to his own proposal, House Bill 328 ("An act to provide for the regulation of the running at large of animals"). The Committee on Herd, Hedge, Fence and Stock Laws reported his bill favorably and sent it to the House for a second reading. There it was sent to the Committee on Judiciary. After that committee recommended its passage, it was adopted by a vote of sixty to ten in the House. But the Senate was dominated by the eastern counties which were less favorable to herd-law proposals. Doster's original bill made the adoption of the provisions of the law optional by the townships. The Senate changed this, making adoption optional at the county level. After adding other amendments designed to cripple the measure, the Senate sent it back to the House. There Doster fought hard for his original measure, but, out of desperation, the House accepted the Senate version. In the final ballot, Doster voted nay.[23]

The act was signed by Governor James M. Harvey on February 24, 1872. In its final form the law empowered the various boards of county commissioners to direct, by an order, which animals could not run at large in their counties. For any destruction caused by straying livestock, the owners of the damaged crops were entitled to a lien against the animals for the full amount of all damages committed. The law further allowed any person to seize those animals specified in the order if the animals appeared to be about to trespass on that person's lands. Despite Doster's apparent disappointment in not having his original proposal passed, the herd law was popular in the areas in which it was adopted and was effective for the brief time it was needed.[24] The law ceased to be necessary when barbed wire became common.

In addition to his attention to the legislation so urgently demanded by his constituency, Doster showed a lively interest in some of the current reform proposals. On February 9, he presented the petition of Samuel N. Wood "on behalf of seven hundred women of Kansas, asking for the right to vote." Wood had been an old free-state radical of the territorial period and was ever eager to embrace reform measures. In presenting the suffrage petition, Doster was displaying for the first time in public his penchant for reform causes and ideas.

Contrary to Doster's request that the petition be sent to the Committee on Judiciary, it was consigned to the Committee on Federal Relations—and oblivion. Later, Representative Goddard introduced a female suffrage bill. When it was proposed that action on the bill be postponed indefinitely, Doster protested. He argued that the bill was as important as any before the House and that its friends should have a fair chance to debate its merits. The *Kansas Commonwealth* of Topeka reported that:

> Mr. Doster said he was perhaps the youngest member of the legislature, but he had lived long enough to know from the whole history of the world that every new step forward had resulted in good and to the best interests of mankind. Without looking at the constitution of the United States, he believed that this law was not against the constitution of Kansas. He recited the clause which gives the right to vote to males, and said it did not say that the females should not vote, and the constitution did not say that the legislature should not by law give them the right to vote. He read from Cooley's constitutional enactments to show that where the constitution did not prohibit a thing that it could do it. The legislature was not expressly or implicited [*sic*] limited, and therefore in accordance with the authority read, it had the power to pass the act.

He cited other authorities, among them a Shawnee County court decision "in which it said that no good lawyer would contend that suffrage was authorized by the constitution or by statute." Referring then to the state's Bill of Rights, which said that all power was inherent in the people, Doster raised the question, "Who is the people?" "When the idea first originated that the people didn't mean women it was at a time when women were under subjection. . . . That reason does not now exist. Women in Kansas now have every right that men does [sic] except voting. When the reason of a construction ceases, the construction itself must cease." In closing, Doster replied to an earlier speaker, who had asserted that the right to vote was not a natural right, by expressing his belief that "the right to vote was as much a natural right as the right to life." The young legislator perhaps made an impression on his listeners, but his cause failed. The motion for indefinite postponement prevailed.[25]

Another reform proposal brought before the legislature was the strengthening of the state's liquor law. Temperance zeal was increasing in Kansas, and the anti-liquor forces succeeded in pushing an amendment through the House designed to put teeth in the Dram Shop Act of 1868. In his early career Doster was a temperance man. He voted for the amendment, which passed the House, but died in the Senate. Another reform measure for which Doster voted, the abolition of capital punishment, likewise passed the House and failed in the Senate.[26] He also worked diligently, with varying success, for legislation of a routine nature.[27]

For a young, inexperienced man, Doster's record was creditable. He showed energy and ability in his first taste of public life. Indeed, he was something of a hero to the "home folks" for his performance in the herd-law fight. The *Record* commented that "Much credit is due Mr. Doster for the energy with which he has labored for the passage of this law, and we deem it an honor to our Representative to have his bill selected as the one possessing the most merit of the large number offered."[28]

Even his espousal of "advanced" notions did not seem to endanger his reputation. There was no discussion of it in the local press. Many of the leading Republicans in the state, moreover, shared his sympathy for equal suffrage; and the temperance movement was gaining momentum throughout Kansas.

Later in 1872 there were other indications that Doster was one of the coming men in Marion County politics. In August he was selected as one of two delegates to the state Republican convention. In the fall, his staunch supporter, editor Charlie Tripplett of the *Record,* endorsed him for district judge. Citing Doster's record in the legislature, the editor believed "it would be but a fitting compliment in return for the inestimable service he performed for the people." In a later issue Tripplett reported Doster's success in securing an injunction against taxation of homestead improvements. The editor took the opportunity to point out that "Mr. Doster is always on the side of the people."[29]

When the Florence *Pioneer* came out in support of the incumbent judge and against Doster's candidacy, a Peabody resident rushed to his defense: "Mr. Doster stands too well in the esteem of the people of western Kansas and has done too much for them as a legislator and lawyer to be injured by such a creature as the editor of the *Pioneer.*"[30]

In mid-October the county Republican convention gave Doster its endorsement. It was becoming apparent that the struggle over the judgeship was little more than an intercounty squabble: incumbent W. R. Brown was a Chase County resident and the Marion Republicans wanted their own man in the office. The *Record* complained that Chase County had a virtual monopoly on all the district offices: "We submit that they are not entitled to three of those offices and Marion have none." The *Record* further charged that Doster's opponent had favored a third term for Grant, whereas Doster "has never been suspicioned of being anything but a straight Republican."[31]

His campaign received another boost when a former officer of the Eleventh Indiana Cavalry, then living in Marion County, wrote in praise of Doster's war record: "His faithful and intelligent performance of duty soon attracted my attention . . . and led me to appoint him a non-commissioned officer in preference to those of more mature years." After describing his conduct during the Tennessee campaign, his former superior concluded his remarks by saying that "the purity of his private life, sterling integrity, industrious habits and legal attainments admirably fit him for the position to which he aspires."[32]

Doster's Marion County support was not enough, however, to carry the election. In November he won only his home county, losing the other four (Chase, Harvey, Reno, and Rice). Although defeated, he was not to be written off politically. He was still quite young and popular with the citizens of his own county.[33]

In the meantime he turned his attention to his private and professional lives. In April of 1873, masons began laying the walls for a new home for his enlarged family (by then he had two children—Lenore and a baby boy, Chase). The house was built on the gentle slope of the east bank of Muddy Creek.[34]

Professionally, he enhanced his reputation with an able defense in a sensational case. His client, Louis Crawford, was convicted in the district court of first-degree murder. Doster appealed the case to the state Supreme Court, winning a reversal and a new trial. The *Record* commented that: "While we depreciated [*sic*] the idea of the county being subjected to the additional cost of another trial, we cannot but admire the energy and pluck of our talented young attorney, the Hon. Frank Doster, counsel for Crawford, who in the face of all the opposition of popular prejudice against his client, and despite the efforts of able attorneys for the state, fought the case bravely." At the second trial, in Emporia, he secured a more favorable verdict for his client—a second-degree conviction and a sentence of twenty-one years of hard labor. The Emporia *News* noted that his arguments were "calm and evinced a maturity of thought rarely found in one so young."[35]

Doster's activities carried him throughout much of Kansas. His "card" in the *Record* told prospective clients he "will practice in Southern Kansas." "Hon. Frank Doster," the local press commented, "is now in Howard County attending to an important law suit. He reports legal business very brisk."[36]

The same article concluded by saying: "He thinks this pays better than politics." But in the fall of 1874, he entered the political arena once more. The county's regular Republicans gave him their endorsement for representative in the legislature. Again a bolting group, this time calling itself the "Farmers' County Ticket," nominated R. C. Bates. In the elections of 1871 and 1873 Doster apparently was held in esteem by the people of Marion County. This time, however, his fellow citizens turned him down; In a quiet election with a light turnout, he was defeated.[37]

Retiring temporarily from politics, Doster nevertheless remained a significant force in his community. Marion Centre, although the county seat, had no railroad. In the summer of 1875 the Marion County Railroad Committee selected Levi Billings and Doster as a committee of two with instructions to confer with the officials of the Santa Fe. The announced goal of the Railroad Committee was a branch line to run from Florence (situated on the main north-south line of the Santa Fe), through Marion Centre and indefinitely westward.

On December 31 the *Record* reprinted a letter to Doster

from five Salina promoters of the branch line. The Salina men urged Doster and Billings to join with them in order to present a united Salina–Marion Centre delegation. The same issue of the *Record* reported a meeting of the combined delegation with the western managers of the Santa Fe. Their efforts did not bear fruit until 1879, when the bonds were finally voted for the Marion & McPherson Railroad, a leased line in the Santa Fe system. The people of Marion Centre were jubilant at the news.[38] The dream that the road would become the new main line, however, was not fulfilled.

Caroline Doster was also active in community affairs. When the ruinous grasshopper invasion of 1874 hit central Kansas, Marion County suffered inordinately from the ravages of the insects, and many citizens were left totally destitute. Carrie served as treasurer of the Marion Centre Relief Society; in that capacity she helped distribute the food, clothing, and other provisions donated by the eastern part of the country.[39]

One Marion Centre professional man came perilously close to financial ruin as a result of the grasshopper plague. Edward Wallis Hoch was a young printer, late of Kentucky, who purchased the *Marion County Record* at the time of the invasion. Like Doster, he was an Ohio Valley product, of a pro-Union, antislavery family, and a straight Republican. Intellect and diligence led him out of the threatened disaster of that summer and eventually propelled him into a position of prominence in Kansas journalism. In time he became the "boss-buster" governor in the Progressive period. He was also to become Doster's most important political foe.

The winter of 1875 found Doster again seeking political favor. His old opponent W. R. Brown resigned his judgeship to take a seat in Congress. In an effort to get the appointment to fill the judicial vacancy, Doster busied himself in rounding up the support of other attorneys in the district. In a series of letters to veteran radical Samuel N. Wood, the ambitious young lawyer demanded Wood's aid in brusk tones: "I want you to bestir yourself now." Other aspirants were equally active and S. R. Peters of Marion emerged as his major rival. In a letter recommending Peters another Marion man told Governor Osborne that Doster was "of a very vindictive malicious disposition." Peters (later a congressman himself) received the position in March. "Mr. Doster," wrote E. W. Hoch, "made a prominent contest and no doubt yields the palm gracefully to the successful man."[40]

A year later the *Record* reprinted a Doster-for-Congress "puff" from the Columbus (Kansas) *Courier*:

> We doubt if there is a man of brighter intellect, or more ability, in the Third district for the position. . . . Our acquaintance with him dates from Hoosierdom. We knew the family. Alfred Doster, the father of Frank, was an uncompromising Union man. He gave three sons to the army, of which Frank only lived to get home. We soldiered with Frank Doster and belonged to the same company and bunked under the same blanket with him. We have watched his course thus far in life and have always found him a good friend, an honest man and we are satisfied if the people of the Third District want to be well and ably represented in Congress, they cannot do better than to send Frank Doster there.[41]

His old comrade's endorsement was to no avail. In fact, there was no real Doster boom; it was his fourth political frustration in three years. Indeed, there is evidence that Doster's popularity was on the wane, although the reasons are not entirely clear.

The following April, editor Hoch leveled a blast at the young attorney entitled "A Frank Talk about Frank Doster." Hoch had been a witness for the prosecution in a slander case in which Doster served as attorney for the defense. In the course of the examination, Hoch found Doster unnecessarily abusive of him and claimed that the lawyer had "passed the pale of his profession and the bounds of a gentleman." This could be dismissed as the rancor of one man, except that the editor went on to say that he was not alone in his disgust with the "young disciple of Blackstone."

> We have shielded him when popular clamor was strong against him. . . . Time after time have we suppressed communications to this paper derogatory to him, and have received on our own head the censure of the correspondents who desired to heap their displeasure upon his. Not only have we withstood this persistent pressure upon the columns of our paper, but have even refused to run our job press in printing charges which had been refused admittance to our paper—in one campaign declining nearly twenty dollars worth of such job work. . . . Mr. Doster only exhibits a pitiable ingratitude when he fails to see any 'moral courage' in an editor thus shielding him from the popular whirlpool threatening to engulf him. . . . He is a poor man indeed who is either morally, mentally or physically afraid of Frank Doster.

Hoch noted too that Doster's own client had once written that the young man "ought to be tarred and feathered." The *Record* editor concluded darkly: "Mr. Doster was once a very popular man in Marion county. He is of course aware of that fact that he has lost that popularity. Why? Did Col. Sam Wood answer that query when he aptly said that Mr. Doster seemed to hold to the theory that a political opponent was necessarily a personal enemy?"[42]

Here were personal allegations—and Hoch was given neither to smear nor sensationalism. It was perhaps with grim satisfaction that he reported another challenge which threatened Doster that spring. At the close of the district court term in June, county attorney L. F. Keller arose and "with an expression of great seriousness" asked leave to present a question of privilege. "All ears were intent as the speaker proceeded to read a sworn accusation against Frank Doster . . . charging him with falsely executing, writing and forging a certain letter as evidence to deceive the court and defeat an action then pending." As Keller took his seat, Doster rose and displayed a readiness to meet the charges. When the court reconvened two days later, he presented an affidavit by himself, swearing that Keller had violated the orders of the court by accompanying a jury to the grounds they were required to inspect. A hearing to air Keller's charge and Doster's counter-accusation was set for July 3.

For reasons not reported, nothing came of the affair. Apparently the disturbing matter was dropped by both men, for there is no mention of it in the *Record*. It was later said, however, that Keller and Doster never spoke to each other again.[43]

The accusation of forgery, whether true or not, did not harm Doster's reputation appreciably. Indeed, he made something of a political comeback. In August the Republicans of the county chose him as a delegate to the state convention, giving him the highest number of votes in a field of five candidates. At the state gathering, the Marion Centre lawyer was honored by being chosen assistant secretary of the convention and a member of the committee on credentials.[44]

It would appear, then, that Doster had survived a series of political defeats and two serious assaults on his professional character. His fortunes seemed on the mend, and he perhaps could have had a satisfactory political career as a regular Republican. Yet it was at this time that he began showing his tendencies towards radicalism, and he displayed them in the boldest possible manner.

In the early 1870's a small group of pious individuals were

agitating for an amendment to the Constitution of the United States which would recognize God as the Supreme Being and Christianity as the national religion. Their crusade received scant notice in the national press; but in the radical journals the matter received a good deal of attention, mostly in the forms of ridicule and denunciation. Among the most vituperative opponents of the proposal were the notorious free-love advocates Victoria Woodhull and Tennie C. Claflin. For several weeks they devoted much space in *Woodhull and Claflin's Weekly* to articles attacking the movement.

In the April 11, 1874, issue of the *Weekly,* there appeared a piece entitled "God and the Constitution," with a Marion Centre dateline and signed by Frank Doster. The writer began by acknowledging the necessity of knowing the attitude of the Founding Fathers towards recognition of the Deity in the Constitution. According to Doster, "The fact that no such recognition was given place in the Constitution argues at least one thing, and that is, that the authors of that compact deemed it unwise and inimical to the free institutions they were then founding to legalize and perpetuate any religious dogma or superstition, and the reason they deemed it so cannot be otherwise than that they were the skeptics and infidels that their sympatheic followers of to-day claim them to have been." He added that the House Committee on Judiciary, to which the proposed amendment was sent, likewise found that the framers had "with unanimity" rejected official recognition of the Deity and Christianity because the principle was antagonistic to a free government. Doster admitted that the argument could only be proven by an examination of the records of the debates of the Constitutional Convention, and they could only be seen by visiting the federal archives. Yet there was a source, readily available to all, which would show conclusively that

23

the statesmen of the early republic opposed a national religion. He cited the *United States Statutes at Large* in which was printed the 1796 treaty between the United States and Tripoli. In that document the Americans affirmed that "the government of the United States of America is not in any sense founded on the Christian religion." Doster concluded that the treaty as "an expression of governmental principle is in direct contradiction to the oft-repeated assertions that all law derives its origin from religion, and that Christianity is part of the common law of the land."

Here Doster was displaying publicly for the first time all the techniques he was to use throughout his career as a radical idealogue. It was not *what* Doster was saying that placed him with the radicals; It was the manner in which he said it. The great majority of the American people were opposed or indifferent to the recognition of God or Christianity in the Constitution. Moreover, he aligned himself squarely with the Federalist fathers and the members of the House Committee on Judiciary of the Republican Congress of 1874. His major arguments were rooted in the Anglo-American legal and constitutional traditions. What was radical about his stand? Nothing. Yet in sending his article to a free-love journal he made himself vulnerable to charges to be made later that he was a believer in sexual license as well as an atheist.[45] When "God and the Constitution" appeared in print, however, it received no comment from the local press.

Likewise, his first assertion of radical thoughts to a local audience did not elicit an unfavorable reaction. At the Fourth of July celebration at Florence in 1878, Doster presented the main address; his theme was inequality in contemporary society. He began by citing three examples of injustice: the liquor dealer's disregard of injury to his victims; public disregard of Chinese rights in California; and the unfairness of capitalists in the wages paid to labor. Then Doster laid down two principles: first, that "no man has the right to take advantage, either directly or indirectly, of the necessities of another, and entrenched and fortified behind the law compel him to accept alternatives;" and secondly, that "The nearer power resided to the people the safer is their government, and the better their liberties are protected."

Certainly most of his hearers would have found nothing repugnant in his remarks thus far. He continued, however, with a discussion of the Paris Commune. Generally, his wording was cautious: "Let our position be not misrepresented. We do not defend the communistic element in politics; we offer only an apology for it. It is the inevitable result of a violation of the eternal laws of individual equality. It is the indignant protest of the masses against the existence of exercise of aristocratic power, and when aroused manifests itself the same as any other revolutionary element in the commission of wild excesses." Doster then directed his audience's attention to the lack of equality in their own country. Although he admitted that neither the Declaration of Independece nor the Constitution guaranteed it, equality was the "unwritten law [which] exists in every man's heart, and is part of God's eternal plan of life."

Again Doster was voicing nothing particularly offensive; and the press reaction was laudatory. E. W. Hoch reported that the speech was "highly complimented." The Florence *Herald* found it "well delivered" and stated that Doster had "put forth new ideas which our people were not aware of."

Later, however, when politics became warmer, opponents were to seize on his "apology" for the Paris Commune. Clearly Doster meant to denote "explanation," but his enemies would quote him out of context, making "apology" synonymous with "defense." Perhaps Doster was only careless in his choice of nouns; or perhaps this might have been another example of his perverse habit of presenting relatively innocuous interpretations in a manner designed to make them seem radical.[46]

In the Kansas of the 1870's, a man with radical proclivities was under no compulsion to find a political attachment outside the Republican party. Republicanism in Kansas had a virtual monopoly of votes and offices, but there was room for dissent and nonconformity. Many a politician enjoyed office, prestige, and popularity despite unorthodox leanings—Congressman William A. Phillips was a conspicuous example. Indeed, cheap money, land-law reform, opposition to monopoly, and sympathy for labor were respectable stands in the eyes of most Kansans.

Despite the latitudinarian nature of Kansas Republicanism, Doster, by 1878, was not content with being identified with the respectable majority. On July 5, the day after his Florence address, he accepted the nomination for attorney general from the Greenback convention at Emporia. In the month following he was honored with a second nomination; the Greenback convention for the Third District, held at Florence, made him its candidate for Congress. Doster captured the nomination on the second ballot, beating the old radical Sam Wood by a vote of forty to nineteen.[47]

However aggravating economic conditions may have been in Kansas, the majority of the people did not find Greenbackism an acceptable solution. Neither Doster nor the other candidates for state and national office were expected to win; local press reaction against his candidacy was accordingly negligible. Hoch of the *Record* was even complimentary when Doster was being nominated for attorney general: "Mr. Doster has the requisite ability to fill the office, and if he accepts will poll a good vote in Marion county." Editorial opposition to him was mild or nonexistent—with one exception. William A. Morgan, editor of the *Chase County Leader,* seized on Doster's hitherto ignored utterances in *Woodhull and Claflin's Weekly* and the Florence address to point out his "free-love" sympathies and "apology" for the Paris Commune. Morgan, a dedicated conservative, fulminated against Doster throughout the campaign. He quoted the Emporia *Sun* which accused Doster of planting himself "squarely on the Democratic side while standing upon the Greenback platform." Doster, according to Morgan, was the choice of the eastern part of the congressional district and Chase County's own Sam Wood had a better chance of getting elected. "Had Ryan [the Republican incumbent] controlled that convention," Morgan grumbled, "he could not have controlled it more to his own interests." Doster was, moreover, "a theorist and not practical and will carry no enthusiasm with the campaign." Morgan's opposition is significant for he was the first influential figure in central Kansas to take strong exception to Doster's views. He remained a bitter critic of the radical lawyer for the remainder of his long career as a newspaperman.[48]

Doster made a surprisingly good showing in his congressional race. In losing, he out-polled the Democratic candidate and was particularly strong in the southeastern portion of the district. He received a strong vote in Marion, Butler, Chatauqua, and Osage counties. The victorious Ryan received only a plurality in Greenwood and Summer counties. In Elk County, Doster had a majority.

He fared less well in the attorney general contest, running well behind the ticket. He did, however, carry Rush County and polled a good vote in Brown, Johnson, Ottawa, Phillips,

Pottawatomie, Reno, Riley, Sedgwick, and Smith counties. In Franklin County, the Republican candidate had only a plurality.[49]

By the end of the 1870's, the Greenback movement had run its course in Kansas and Doster shifted his allegiance to the Union Labor party shortly after the 1878 campaign. He was not to make another race for a decade.[50]

Although out of politics, his interest in radical ideology flourished. It was no longer a flirtation with heterodoxy, but a wholehearted embracing of reform thought. In 1879 both Doster and his wife became associated with the National Liberal League. The Liberal League, which claimed over two hundred local auxiliaries in Kansas alone, was dedicated to the total separation of church and state. Among its cardinal tenets were opposition to the following: use of the Bible in public schools, public suport of sectarian schools and charitable institutions, official recognition of religious holidays, and the judicial oath.

A national meeting of the League was held at Bismarck Grove, near Lawrence, from the fifth to the tenth of September. The Dosters played a prominent role in the gathering. Frank was a member of the preparatory committee and Carrie was treasurer of the state organization. The five-day meeting was devoted largely to speeches against church control over secular life. Curiously, several leading Kansas Republicans were also identified with the Liberal movement. Other members of the preparatory committee were: Charles Robinson, first governor of the state; D. R. Anthony, Leavenworth publisher and a fiery Republican; Sol Miller of the Kansas *Chief* (Troy), a Republican stalwart from territorial days; George R. Peck, the leading Kansas attorney for the Santa Fe; and F. P. Baker, editor and publisher of the Topeka *Common-*

wealth. The only non-Republicans on the committee were Doster, Annie L. Diggs (later an important Populist agitator), and U. F. Sargent, editor of the Fort Scott *Pioneer.*

The Dosters' association with the League was apparently short-lived and did not arouse much press comment at the time—even though it could have strengthened the "atheist" charge so frequently hurled at him. As can be seen by the number of distinguished Republicans with whom he served, dissent could be respectable.[51]

In fact, Doster was reputable enough to be called to Washington the following year to testify before a Senate committee investigating the recent "Exodus" of southern Negroes to northern states. Kansas had been inundated by these destitute immigrants, whose suffering was great, and state officials were hard-pressed to provide relief and work for them. In Washington the affair was a political football. The Democrats were determined to demonstrate that the Exodus and its unfortunate results were caused by Republican and Negro agitators. The Republicans were equally determined to show that it was a result of deplorable conditions in the South.

Doster appeared before the committee on April 8, 1880. The senators first tried to determine his political loyalties. Doster cautiously stated that he believed his father had been a Douglas Democrat in 1860 and that he himself had been a Republican originally but had voted the Greenback ticket in the last election. "I guess I had better call myself an Independent." Doster also parried questions on his opinions on the reasons for the Exodus. He had talked with a few of the "Exodusters" when in Topeka but "did not make inquiries of a great many as to the causes of their leaving the South." He added cryptically, "I had my own opinion about that. . . ." Doster further avoided voicing his views on the background of the immigration by expressing his concern for the immigrants' predicament in Kansas. There, he said, it was difficult even for white men to find work. He told the committee that he believed the need for cheap railroad construction labor might create employment for the Negroes. Again the committeemen tried to draw him out by asking him whether in his opinion "it would not be better for the government . . . to protect these people where they are, than for them to go to Kansas seeking employment?" Doster warily replied that "it would be much better for them to be protected, if they need protection, where they are now, than for them to come to Kansas."

In response to further interrogation Doster expressed his belief that the prevailing sentiment in Kansas was against the migration: "Our means are limited, and it is all we can do to take care of ourselves. For this reason, I think this class of negroes is not generally desired by our citizens." He concluded by saying that he did not believe that the Exodus was to the advantage of the Negroes, either.[52]

Doster's evasive attitude makes it impossible to know his true feelings on the questions foremost in the minds of his interrogators. Clearly he opposed the immigration into his state, but his attitude towards southern conditions is unclear. Subsequent utterances, however, showed him to be in sympathy with the Negroes, northern and southern.

Kansas in the prosperous eighties was little suited for a career in radical politics. Doster accordingly devoted most of his time to his two abiding loves—his family and the law. Shortly after his arrival in Kansas his daughter Lenore was born. A year later Carrie bore him a son, Chase. The Dosters lost two sons, Karl (1875), who died at the age of four, and Hume (1879), who died in infancy. Two other sons and a daughter survived childhood and brought the total to five: Wade (1880), John (1889), and Irma (1893).[53]

In the 1870's Carrie's brothers Taylor and Leon Riddle emigrated from Illinois to Marion. With them came their mother and a younger sister who later committed suicide. Their father also prepared to join them, but died in 1876.[54]

Doster's close attention to his profession earned him a busy and lucrative practice. He was now professionally mature and becoming a lawyer's lawyer, and even his bitterest political enemies of later years credited him with much ability. He was, moreover, genuinely in love with the law. A charter member of the state bar association (organized in 1883), Doster served on its first executive council. Even in the tumultuous 1890's, he continued to be an active member of various committees of the association.[55]

Socially Doster was almost a complete outsider. A careful search of the local newspapers reveals no mention of membership in any club or lodge. Seldom is his name found among those attending the community's many social gatherings; nor was he a church member. His reserve and aloofness gave him the reputation of being cold and forbidding. The Kansas poet Eugene F. Ware later branded him "bloodless Doster."[56] His slender, slope-shouldered frame and unsmiling, parchment-like face made it easy for opponents to emphasize his frigid manner. There is evidence that Doster was a shy man with a total inability to be a "good fellow." Perhaps his devotion to family and profession left little time for mingling with others. Perhaps his intellectual bent and radicalism also played a part in keeping him from the company of his fellow citizens.

His Civil War experiences influenced him, however, to become an early and zealous member of the local post of the Grand Army of the Republic. Excepting the bar association, the GAR was the only organization to which he gave his life-long support.[57]

Doster's fascination with the military also led to a brief career in the militia. In the spring of 1884 a local infantry company was mustered into the Second Regiment of the Kansas Militia, with Doster as its captain.[58]

In the 1880's one of the primary responsibilities of the militia was to suppress the many county-seat "wars" of the western portion of the state. The most serious of these, the Stevens County disturbance of 1888, gave Marion's D Company and its commander a chance for service. The company was called out by Governor John A. Martin, along with the other units of the regiment, to bring peace to the far-western county. The rival towns of Hugoton and Woodsdale were engaged in a particularly heated struggle involving actual bloodshed. The leader of the Woodsdale faction was the town's founder, Sam Wood—twice Doster's political opponent, but also his friend.

Doster's adoring daughter Irma wrote a colorful account of the affair which gave her father almost sole credit for restoring peace. Her melodramatic story shows Captain Doster appearing unarmed before a whiskey-crazed Hugoton mob, defying them by baring his chest and daring them to shoot. Another thrilling sequence has Doster—again unarmed—confronting Sam Wood and demanding successfully that he surrender his pistol. The official reports of the "war" do not acknowledge these heroics; nor does a later scholarly history of the fracas mention that Doster played a prominent role in its suppression. The *Cottonwood Valley Times* of Marion printed some mock-serious "war correspondence" which indicated that the local boys looked on their Stevens County soldiering as a lark.[59]

County-seat wars were commonplace in Kansas during the 1880's. The wars were an element of the town-booming phenomenon of the decade. Securing the county seat was the first step in building the "new Chicago." The booming movement collapsed as a world-wide depression set in. The economic disorder did much to further the political rise of Frank Doster and other Kansas radicals.

NOTES

[1]Mrs. Ben Hill Doster, *The Doster Genealogy* (Richmond: The William Byrd Press, 1945), pp. xi and 56; Frank Doster, "Eleventh Indiana Cavalry in Kansas in 1865," *Kansas Historical Collections,* XV (1919–22), 524–25*n*.

[2]Mrs. Ben Hill Doster, *Doster Genealogy,* pp. 53 and 63; Topeka *Mail,* Sept. 5, 1896; Frank Doster, "Eleventh Indiana Calvary in Kansas," pp. 524–25*n*; Alfred F. Doster Military Records, File XC2656197, National Archives.

[3]Mrs. Ben Hill Doster, *Doster Genealogy,* pp. 53 and 56; Alfred F. Doster Military Records.

[4]Frank Doster, "Eleventh Indiana Cavalry in Kansas," p. 524.

[5]*Ibid.,* pp. 524–25.

[6]*Ibid.,* p. 525.

[7]*Ibid.,* p. 526.

[8]*Ibid.,* pp. 527–29.

[9]Alfred F. Doster Military Records; Marion *Review,* Sept. 10, 1941.

[10]Frank Doster, "Eugene V. Debs," address, *ca.* 1926, Doster MSs, University of Kansas Library; Mrs. Ben Hill Doster, *Doster Genealogy,* p. 63; Frank Doster, "Eleventh Indiana Cavalry," p. 525*n*; James C. Malin, *A Concern about Humanity: Notes on Reform, 1872–1912, at the National and Kansas Levels of Thought* (Lawrence, Kansas: The Author, 1964), p. 132; Marion *Review,* Sept. 10, 1941.

[11]Marion *Review,* Sept. 10, 1941.

[12]Kansas State Board of Agriculture, *Third Annual Report* (Topeka: 1874), pp. 168–69.

[13]Marion *Review,* Sept. 10, 1941.

[14]S. R. Peters, "Old Ninth Judicial District; Incidents and Suggestions," *Proceedings of the Twenty-fifth Annual Meeting of the Bar Association of the State of Kansas* (Topeka: 1908), p. 145.

[15]*Marion County Record,* Oct. 5 and Dec. 16, 1871, and Jan. 4, 1872; Paul Wallace Gates, *Fifty Million Acres: Conflicts over Kansas Land Policy, 1854–1890* (Ithaca, New York: Cornell University Press, 1954), p. 236.

[16]Marion *Review,* Sept. 10, 1941.

[17]See Rodney Owen Davis, "The Fencing Problem and the Herd Law in Kansas, 1855–1883" (unpublished Master's thesis, University of Kansas, 1959).

[18]*Marion County Record,* Oct. 21 and Nov. 4, 1871; *Annual Report of the Secretary of State of the State of Kansas* (Topeka: 1871), p. 26.

[19]*House Journal: Proceedings of the Legislative Assembly of the State of Kansas, Twelfth Annual Session* (Topeka: 1872), pp. 85, 212, and 131–32 (hereafter cited as *House Journal*).

[20]*Marion County Record,* Jan. 20, 1872.

[21]*Ibid.,* Jan. 27, 1872.

[22]*Ibid.; House Journal,* pp. 365 and 531–32.

[23]*House Journal,* pp. 423, 426, 447, 468, 473, 527–28, and 945–46.

[24]*Ibid.,* p. 1010; *Laws of Kansas,* 1872 (Topeka: 1872), pp. 384–85; Kansas State Board of Agriculture, *Fourth Annual Report* (Topeka: 1875), p. 327.

[25]*House Journal,* pp. 606, 607, and 1047; (Topeka) *Kansas Commonwealth,* Feb. 28, 1872.

[26]William E. Connelley, *A Standard History of Kansas and Kansans* (Chicago: Lewis Publishing Co., 1918), II, 804; *Kansas Commonwealth,* Feb. 14, 1872; *House Journal,* pp. 1128–29.

[27]*House Journal,* pp. 764, 1151–53, 1278, 281, 920, and 105; U. S. Senate, 42d Cong., 2d Sess., *Resolution in Relation to the Removal of Settlers from the Indian Territory, Bordering upon Kansas, and also in Favor of a Change of Boundaries of Said State,* Senate Misc. Doc. 49 (Washington: 1872).

[28]*Marion County Record,* Feb. 10, 1872.

[29]*Ibid.,* Aug. 31, Sept. 14, and Oct. 5, 1872.

[30]*Ibid.,* Oct. 12, 1872.

[31]*Ibid.,* Oct. 19 and Nov. 2, 1872.

[32]*Ibid.,* Nov. 2, 1872.

[33]*Annual Report of the Secretary of State,* 1872 (Topeka: 1873), p. 28.

[34]Quoted in the *Marion County Record,* April 5, 1873; Marion *Review,* Sept. 10, 1941.

[35]Quoted in the *Marion County Record,* Aug. 23, 1873.

[36]*Ibid.,* Aug. 8 and Oct. 18, 1873.

[37]*Ibid.,* Oct. 31 and Nov. 7, 1874.

[38]*Ibid.,* Sept. 3 and Dec. 31, 1875.

[39]*Ibid.,* Jan. 30, 1875; Marion *Record-Review,* Jan. 16, 1947.

[40]Doster to Wood, Dec. 14, 1874, Jan. 6, and Jan. 18, 1875, S. N. Wood MSs, Manuscripts Division, Kansas State Historical Society; Lemuel D. Dobbs to Thomas A. Osborne, Jan. 28, 1875, Governors' Correspondence, Gov. Osborne, Box 1, "Applications, Endorsements and Remonstrances, 1873–1876," Archives Division, Kansas State Historical Society; *Marion County Record,* March 13, 1875.

[41]*Ibid.,* April 7, 1876.

[42]*Ibid.,* April 28, 1876.

[43]*Ibid.,* June 16, 1876; *Biographical Clippings,* D, III (Kansas State Historical Society), p. 305.

[44]*Marion County Record,* Aug. 11, 1876; Malin, *A Concern about Humanity,* p. 133.

[45]Malin, *Ibid.*

[46]*Ibid.,* 134–37; *Marion County Record,* July 5, 1878; Florence *Herald,* July 6, 1878.

[47]Malin, p. 138; D. W. Wilder, *Annals of Kansas* (Topeka: T. D. Thatcher, 1886), p. 801.

[48]Malin, p. 138; *Chase County Leader,* Aug. 29 and Oct. 3, 1878.

[49]Malin, pp. 138–39.

[50]Kansas City *Star,* Nov. 29, 1896.

[51]Malin, pp. 64–65 and 139.

[52]U. S. Senate, 46th Cong., 2d Sess., *Report and Testimony of the Select Committee of the United States Senate to Investigate the Causes of the Removal of the Negroes from the Southern States to the Northern States,* Senate Report 693, pt. 3 (Washington: 1880), pp. 105–07.

[53]Mrs. Ben Hill Doster, *Doster Genealogy,* pp. 56–57.

[54]L. H. Riddle, MS Diary, 1887–1891, microfilm copy at Kansas State Historical Society, pp. 3–4.

[55]*Bar Association of the State of Kansas, Proceedings* (Topeka: 1886), p. 62.

[56]"Governor Lewellings's Farewell Address," unidentified newspaper clipping, Eugene Fitch Ware MSs, University of Kansas Library.

[57]Grand Army of the Republic, Headquarters Department of Kansas, *General Orders No. 5, Wardell Administration, Series 1932–1933* (Topeka: 1933).

[58]Adjutant General of the State of Kansas, *Fourth Biennial Report* (Topeka: 1884), p. 25; *Ibid., Fifth Biennial Report* (1886), p. 80.

[59]Irma Doster, *Freedom has a Happy Ring: A Kansas Bulletin for Kansas Schools* (Topeka: Burge Printing Co., 1960), pp. 38–39; Joseph W. Snell, "The Stevens County Seat War" (unpublished Master's thesis, University of Kansas: 1962); *Cottonwood Valley Times,* Aug. 9, 1888.

2

THE RIGHTS OF THE USER

THE TOWN of Marion (shortened from "Marion Centre" in 1881), like many communities in central Kansas, aspired to be an important city. Even level-headed community leaders like E. W. Hoch caught the booming fever and joined in the agitation for the development of industry, commerce, and transportation.

A few successes inflated their hopes. In 1885, a bond issue was voted to bring the Omaha, Abilene, and Wichita line (of the Rock Island system) to Marion. Among the attempts to make the village an industrial center were the establishment of a brick works, a sorghum factory, an iron foundry, and a creamery. The boomers also undertook the construction of hotels, resorts, bridges, better streets, and more houses. Local promoters distributed a pamphlet advertising the agricultural glories and bright commercial prospects of Marion County. Waters to the northeast of Marion were found to possess marvelous curative powers and Chingawasa Springs became an integral part of the booming movement. By 1889, the Marion Belt and Chingawasa Railroad was completed, allowing excursionists easy access to the prairie spa. Plans were under way for boat and bath houses as well as a restaurant and hotel.[1]

Frank Doster did not escape the speculative fever of the flush times of the eighties. Although a radical in political and social thought and a cautious man in matters of personal finance, he was busily engaged in buying town lots and farm properties. Leon Riddle's diary mentions the transfer of four lots from his mother to Frank and Carrie Doster in 1887. In another entry Riddle tells of writing a lease for his brother-in-law since "he [Doster] is renting one of his farms to a Russian." Doster also purchased lots for himself and members of his family from the Marion Town Company, an organization formed by local boomers. Two cases brought before the state Supreme Court show that he was buying property in nearby Peabody through tax deeds.[2]

Kansas in the prosperous and optimistic eighties offered scant opportunities to the radicals. Doster was accordingly silent on political matters throughout most of the decade. He did, however, continue to make speeches to local audiences. In December of 1885 he was scheduled to make an address before the Chase County chapter of the Irish National League; but, being unable to meet the appointment, he sent a letter of regret in which he expressed sympathy for the Irish cause. His association with the League should not be taken as evidence of radicalism, since anti-British, pro-Irish sentiment was widespread in Kansas.[3] On Declaration Day in 1887 he delivered an oration at Canton. The newspaper there reported that "The address was a masterly one, superior from a literary and philosophical point of view to any Memorial Day address that has appeared in print so far in the state. It will bear careful study." That same summer he made the Fourth of July speech at Strong City. Apparently it too contained no offensive or explosive matter, for there was no adverse press commentary.[4]

Politically he was inactive, belonging to no party. His brother-in-law Taylor Riddle was active in Republican politics. In 1884, Riddle was vice-president of the local Blaine and Logan club. Three years later he was chairman of Marion's Republican central committee and toying with the notion of running for sheriff.[5]

The booming spirit and relative political complacency were to come to an abrupt end before the close of the eighties. Even before the collapse of the boom, seeds of dissatisfaction were being sown among the Kansas farmers. The boom was primarily a town affair for, along with the emphasis on the promotion of industry and an urbanized social life, there was an attendant lack of concern for the farmers and their problems.[6] Certainly editor Hoch was guilty of ignoring the needs of the farmer in this period. In the 1870's he had devoted much space in the *Record* to news of crops, discussions of improving tillage, and reports of the social life of rural Marion County. In the next decade he dropped the columns of news from the agricultural townships, replacing them with reports of the brilliant prospects of the town. Nor was Doster, with his land and town-lot speculation, doing anything to mitigate the pernicious effects of the boom.

The giddy hopes of the specultors and town promoters were dashed by 1887. A depression which was to plague Kansas and the nation for the next ten years had begun. The diary of Leon Riddle for the years 1887–1891 offers a remarkably close look at the economic and psychological effects of the depression. During this period Riddle failed as a farmer, town-lot speculator, and merchant. A few entries from his diary suffice to show the local conditions which gave rise to the protest movement in which his brother-in-law was to take a prominent part.

[July 30, 1887] I am harder up for money than I ever was in my life. I stood around the streets all day wondering what kind of turn I could make to raise some money. The crop prospects are so blue & there is no confidence in Real Estate. You can't sell anything.

[August 23, 1888] The old inhabitants say money is closer than it was grasshopper year (1874) [.] Everyone is so badly in debt when they were not then. If it was not for *interest,* to say nothing about principal we could squeeze along, but a great many are giving up & move that will. J. H. Buchanan our largest Dry Goods Merchant announced his intention of moving his stock to Colorado. Such things have a bad influence. He will sell at cost for 30 days before going.

[September 8, 1888] A great many covered wagons pass through here going East [.] The majority of people in western Kansas are leaving. They have had very poor or no crops at all for 2 & 3 years & are compelled to leave.

[February 12, 1890] There is a great deal of complaint of very hard times. Everything the farmer has to sell is so cheap. Corn about 12¢, oats, 15, Hay 2.50 delivered in town, Eggs 10¢ all winter. And wheat about 50¢ per bus[hel]—and of course when this is the case the hard times are sure to be close.

According to the entry for February 23, 1888, Doster, too, was experiencing financial difficulty: "Frank Doster owes me $50 but can't pay it till next month."

Riddle's bewilderment and despair led him at times to ponder the causes of poverty and question the capitalistic system:

[August 16, 1889] Financial want, or the condition in which you constantly fear the results of poverty is a great source of unhappiness, and such a large per cent of people are either in actual want of the necessities of life, or are in a condition that a little misfortune financially or physically would put them in that condition, that it is no wonder we should be led to doubt the equality of advantages from our present social system & live in the hope of a bettered condition in the future. While it is true that almost everything is cheaper now than in the past, it is also true that the cost of living is increasing, because the standard of respectability has risen: peoples wants are constantly increasing with increased production. What would have been considered comparative comfort in the mode of living 100 years ago, would now be looked at as almost abject poverty in many cases. When we look at the inequalities that have grown up between the two classes, the rich & the poor, in the last 100 years, & consider that such a radical change cannot continue for a similar period with out reducing the masses to a condition of slavery or worse, it is evident that some great change has got to take place in our social system in the future. Just what it will be, or what would really be for the best in the majority of cases can only be ascertained by experience. While I think it is evident that many of the theories suggested by the social theorists are plausible & would be greatly advantageous to the majority, still the great question arises[,] can we educate the people up to the standard necessary for the successful operation of these various changes?

His concern over social and economic maladjustments caused him to do much thinking and reading on reform. He was impressed with Tolstoy's *What Is to Be Done?*, in which the Russian argued that social ills were the result of allowing too many people to live without working. On the other hand, he was less favorable to the analysis and solutions offered in one of the early protest works of the Populist movement, William A. Peffer's *The Way Out*. Peffer's statistics, Riddle thought, proved nothing.[7]

Riddle noted the rise and growth of protest organizations in the area. In 1888 only the Union Labor party was advocating a bold program. "I attended a Union Labor Speech this evening. I was ignorant of the principles advocated by them, before attending the speech. They have just cause for complaint & some of the principles they endorse would be well to become laws."[8]

By 1890, the Farmers' Alliance was the major agrarian protest group in Marion County and elsewhere in Kansas. On February 12, Riddle wrote that bad conditions had "greatly augmented the growth of The 'Farmers Alliance[,]' an organization composed mostly of western farmers, whose objects are to remedy the evils by electing representatives from their own ranks & not so many Bankers & Lawyers as heretofore. A few of their aims are, to do away with so many middlemen, operate stores of their own, on the Co-operative system, each share holder enjoying the priviledges [*sic*] that will result, Reduction of the Tariff, extending the time in which property sold on execution can be redeemed & many other minor objects and aims." On July 15, 1890, he recorded that: "The Farmers Alliance held a picnic today. There was about 5000 people. . . . The largest crowd I think ever in this county. Hon. Ben Terrell, Alliance Lecturer of Texas and Hon. Ralph [Beaumont] of N. Y. Nat'l K[nights] of L[abor] lecturer spoke."

The hard times accentuated specific grievances of many Marion County farmers. Much of the acreage in the northwestern portion of the county had been purchased by an Irish landowner, "Lord" William Scully. After the Civil War, Scully acquired an empire of Kansas, Nebraska, Missouri, and Illinois farm lands. He developed a leasing system which, though not without advantages to the tenants, appeared oppresive in times of economic distress. Anti-Scullyism dominated the agrarian movement in Marion County. Other farmers and even townspeople were in sympathy with the Scully tenants. Their protests eventually made alien landholding a major issue in state politics.[9]

In addition to the tenancy problem, there was the more widespread grievance over interest rates. The *Cottonwood Valley Times* complained of the 2 to 5 percent a month paid by some debtors. "The alleged Scully landlordism is a blessing compared with the practices of some of our money loaners."[10]

In this period of depression and discontent, Frank Doster reentered politics—but not as a radical. Indeed, he was again put into public life under Republican auspicies.

In 1887 the Kansas judiciary was reorganized and expanded. Marion County was in the newly created twenty-fifth Judicial District along with Chase and McPherson counties. Republican Governor John A. Martin was empowered to select judges for the new districts. Members of the Marion County bar began an early and vigorous campaign to have Frank Doster appointed.

On March 6, R. M. Crane, president of the First National Bank of Marion, wrote Martin: "Our bar has prevailed on Mr. Doster to accept the appointment providing it may be satisfactory to the bars of the other co[untie]s. Mr. D. is a lawyer of quite a reputation—one who will be at once recognized as of unquestionable fitness in every way for the place."[11]

A second candidate for the judgeship was Thomas O. Kelly of Cottonwood Falls, who wrote to Martin on March 7, asking to be considered. The following day, however, Kelly withdrew his application, stating that he would never have sought the place had he known that Doster was also a candidate.

Meanwhile, Doster went to Topeka to apply in person. Finding that Martin was in Abilene, he wrote the governor a letter: "If I can secure the appointment to [the] judgeship of [the] 25th Dist. without a contest annoying to myself and embarrassing to you I will be grateful to receive it. . . . If I find that the attorneys of the District favor me for the place as my friends have led me to believe they do, I shall make bold to ask for the appointment." He added that friends would see the governor personally on the matter. Enclosed with Doster's application was Kelly's withdrawal.

With the leading possibilities from the other counties out of the running, Doster's prospects were bright. But on the same day he sent his application, Thomas H. Grisham of Cottonwood Falls wrote Martin requesting the appointment. The next day another member of the Chase County bar informed the governor that the lawyers there were divided on the question of endorsement, but only those lawyers whose primary interest was real estate were backing Grisham. Two other Cottonwood Falls attorneys sent a strong endorsement for Doster: "There are other applicants from this county of ours whom we might be expected to indorse, but in this instance we put aside all such considerations and looking solely to the public interest indorse Frank Doster as in our judgment the most competent of any of the aspirants. He stands above reproach and if any is flung at him it is simply the venting of a petty, narrow and malicious spirit, which ought not to prevail against him—judge him according to his merits and his friends will be satisfied." Among the other letters recommending Doster was that of the judge of the district which had formerly included Marion County. Even attorneys outside the district lent their endorsement to Doster. L. B. Kellogg (later a Republican attorney general) told the governor that he believed him to be "the most competent man in that District for judge."[12]

Clearly, Doster had the backing of most of the district bar, as well as much support from bankers and real-estate men. Yet Grisham refused to yield. In a letter of March 12, he told Governor Martin that the Marion County bar supported his rival simply because he was a resident of the county. He alleged, moreover, that some of the Marion lawyers would not support Doster but had promised not to fight him. In a letter to a Topeka man, whom he asked to intercede with Martin, Grisham wrote: "The man who is opposing me has always been a Greenbacker and never did anything for the Republican party."[13]

Grisham's persistence led Doster's backers to denounce the Cottonwood Falls aspirant. The coroner of Chase County informed Martin that Grisham "is not considered better than a third-rate lawyer with but a very limited practice and that he truckles to the whiskey ring in this community is true beyond a doubt." Thomas O. Kelly told Martin bluntly that Grisham was "wholly incompetent" and that when serving as county attorney he had not enforced prohibition.[14]

Despite the backing of so many respectable and influential men, charges that Doster's political and religious views were less than orthodox would not down. Most of the county officials, the mayor of Marion, a Presbyterian minister, and a banker sent their "testimony of his good character and reputation" and urged the governor to ignore accusations against him.[15]

Their sentiments were echoed in a message to Martin from the manager of the Florence Loan Company. He assured Martin that Doster "voted the Republican ticket and supports Republican principles" and that he was confident that Doster had voted for Blaine in 1884. Nor was he a religious infidel: "I have had several protracted conversations with him on matters pertaining to Religion and am free to say that his views are almost entirely opposite to those generally ascribed to him." The writer conceded, however, that Doster's thoughts on religion were "somewhat liberal."[16]

Even with so many vigorous endorsements, the Governor could have denied the appointment on the grounds of Doster's questionable political loyalty. But Martin, on March 19, awarded the position to the Marion lawyer.[17]

Whatever the talk concerning his peculiar attitudes toward some matters, there was no question about his professional orthodoxy. Earlier that year he had aired his views on "The Relations of Lawyers to Society and their Clients" at the annual meeting of the state bar association. He argued that society was an interested party in any court case and that a lawyer's obligation to it was greater than to his client. Doster emphatically rejected Lord Brougham's dictum that "An advocate in the discharge of his duty knows but one person in all the world, and that person is his client." To Doster the statement was extravagant, absurd, and vicious. The lawyer's overriding concern should be to insure that justice be done, regardless of the effect on his client. A bad decision in any lawsuit harmed society. An attorney was therefore obliged to refuse to be enlisted in the defense of a bad cause. He must of course take every step necessary to protect the rights of a guilty client and make certain that the punishment is not unduly severe; but the lawyer must also protect his ultimate client, society. He must not keep his guilty client from being punished by being more clever, learned, or unscrupulous than the opposing lawyer. Perhaps with reference to the Paris Commune, Doster warned his audience of the consequences of continued injustice: "Within recent memory bloody insurrection ran riot in the streets, and hot flames threatened the homes of a great city, because righteous justice had so long been dethroned in her temples."[18]

His closing remarks were distinctly conservative in tone: "We have no interest in turning felons out to prey upon the communities where we live, and the lawyer who does so by false plea, or artifice, or technical insistence, is an accessory to the crime. My interest and yours are with our homes and neighbors. Our first and highest obligation is to them, to those who look to us as supporters of the social state, as stays and bulwarks against the flood of crime, as guardians of the rights of all."[19]

Despite Doster's known ability and legal conservatism, opposition to his elevation to the bench continued after his appointment. His perennial detractor, W. A. Morgan of the *Chase County Leader,* expressed his bitter opposition to Governor Martin's action in an editorial of March 24. Admitting that Doster was "one of the ablest attorneys in the district" and that he enjoyed "a larger practice than any of his professional brothers," Morgan explained that he opposed the appointment "because we believed him to be cold-blooded, vindictive and influenced by his personal and political hatreds." Morgan asserted that even if Doster was not a believer in communism, he was most certainly "an apologist for the crimes committed under that name." Likewise, if he was not a practitioner of free love, he had defended the actions and doctrines of Victoria Woodhull. He accused the new judge of saying that he would have voted for Cleveland in 1884, but since he lived in Kansas, he cast his ballot for John P. St. John, the Prohibition party's candidate.

Finally, Morgan believed that not one of ten lawyers who supported Doster's candidacy believed him fit for the bench. Two-thirds of his supporters wanted him out of practice so they might increase their own. The other one-third signed the petitions because they were afraid to refuse. Two weeks later Morgan directed his fire at the editors who had approved the appointment, accusing them of "toadyism."[20]

Traditionally, district judges were elected on a nonpartisan basis. The majority of the editors, lawyers, and politicians in the three counties were content to let Doster run unopposed for reelection. In August, Hoch expressed indignation over a scheme by certain Republicans to defeat the incumbent judge. This provoked a blast from Morgan who called the Marion *Record* "the Doster organ of that town." He also vented his anger at the Republican leadership of Marion County because they opposed the calling of a judicial nominating convention. "Such a procedure has a tendency to make a judgeship a life holding. . . . It is an almost monarchial position under such circumstances. . . . A few months of Judge Doster's reign has shown the fear many people have of offending the Judge, who they fear will injure them if they oppose his known wishes."[21]

The only other newspapers of importance to join the anti-Doster forces were the Peabody *Gazette,* Marion *Register,* and McPherson *Freeman.* The others, including Democratic organs such as the *Cottonwood Valley Times,* stood by the Judge. Most of the district's bar also continued to favor him. Early in September, ten Republican and six Democratic lawyers of McPherson County published an appeal to Doster to place his name before the people. Their request was seconded by an open letter from the county's clerk of the court and the sheriff.[22]

Since it was customary to keep the election of judges out of party politics, the delicate question of the Judge's religion was debated more than his political affiliation. The *Cottonwood Valley Times* labeled the charge of atheism "utterly false" and stated that Doster had "given as liberally to churches and similar institutions, according to his means, as any man in Marion County." Editor Hoch wrote that Doster was a skeptic but not an atheist; nor was he a disbeliever in God or immortality.[23]

Western Marion County and eastern McPherson County had been settled by deeply religious German-Russian Mennonites. Among them the "atheist" charge could carry much weight. Fortunately for Doster, the editor of the *Marion County Anzeiger* denied that the Judge had no religious faith and urged his fellow Mennonites to give him their votes. An old, respected Marion resident, R. C. Coble, also tried to dispel the rumor that Doster was an infidel. In a letter to the *Cottonwood Valley Times,* Coble wrote that while Doster earlier had "no fixed convictions" on matters of religion, the death of one of his children had led him to study the question of the immortality of the soul.[24]

In response to the "flattering terms" of appeals to him, Doster announced his candidacy formally on September 16. Four days later the anti-Doster forces met at an irregular judicial convention in McPherson. There they nominated M. P. Simpson of that city to oppose the incumbent.[25]

The Judge may have had the support of most of his colleagues and other influential men in the three counties, but he had made bitter enemies. Also, his personal aloofness kept him from being popular with his fellow citizens. Late in October, Leon Riddle confided to his diary that "The contest between him and M. P. Simpson is close." In another entry he wrote that after hearing Simpson speak he was sure that Doster was the better orator. As the election drew closer he recorded that "Politics is all the rage now. The contest between Frank Doster and M. P. Simpson is probably going to be close. It is exciting & is being fought hard on both sides." On the eve of election day he wrote: "Politics are very warm. Men can be seen gathered in groups, discussing the Judicial question at all hours." On election day, he was confident: "There has been a great excitement & a heavy vote polled. The indications are good that Frank is elected."[26]

Riddle's optimism was justified. When the votes were

counted he learned that his brother-in-law had triumphed: "Frank Doster's majority in the three counties is probably about 1600⁰⁰ [sic]. He carried McPherson City & carried the ward Simpson lives in. They are burning bonfires this evening." Doster's actual majority was 1,760. He carried McPherson County 2,367 to 1,556 and Chase 1,336 to 723. His majority in his home county, however, was relatively slight; he received only 1,929 votes to Simpson's 1,593. His ardent supporters were nevertheless jubilant; after the election, around three dozen of them from throughout the district held an impromptu gathering at Marion's Elgin Hotel where they offered their congratulations to the victor.[27]

In the first years of his term those who had supported him showed no regrets. In 1888, Hoch noted in the *Record* that "Mr. Doster is making an able, dignified, impartial and just judge." When the Judge fined two lawyers ten dollars apiece for shouting "liar" at each other, the *Cottonwood Valley Times* applauded his action.[28]

While he was gaining respect as a jurist, Doster was also enhancing his reputation as an orator. Leon Riddle's diary contains a short synopsis of his brother-in-law's 1890 Declaration Day address at the local opera house.

> He made a very nice speech. It was much beyond the ordinary, he went into the philosophy & historical events to show how strifes were necessary to promote loyalty & cement the feelings of the people as a nation. That the civil war was fought for a principal [sic] vital to the interests of civilization. It was whether people should dwell together in peace as a whole or whether they should live in separate states & such a result would have had a [harmful] influence on civilization, whereas now it has been demonstrated to the world that a Republican form of government is a success & will & is being followed by other nations of the earth.[29]

Inadequate though Riddle's reporting may be, two facts are evident. First, even as the agrarian movement was approaching high tide, Frank Doster was not espousing radical political views. Secondly, his speech of 1890 shows that he was imbibing fully the hypernationalism of the day and all its militaristic overtones. As the century was drawing to a close, members of the Civil War generation expressed alarm at the decadence of the age and the moral and spiritual flabbiness of the younger men. Many of them attributed the decay to the absence of war. War, they believed, "redeemed" society by cleansing it of impurities; strife brought out the nobler, more manly qualities. It is perhaps significant that this heightened militarism immediately preceded the aggression against Spain and the rise of Theodore Roosevelt.[30]

Doster's 1890 speech, however, was not an extreme expression of his militarism. Hoch, who was decidedly opposed to the glorification of war, found nothing objectionable in the Judge's statements and remarked that Doster was "one of the finest orators in Kansas."[31] In the following year, however, Doster gave a Strong City audience a full-blown eulogy on war and warriors. The occasion was the annual celebration of Robert Emmet Day (March 4). Although he entitled the address "Irishmen in American Wars," his remarks largely concerned the beneficial effects of war. "In all ages and climes . . . war has been the most interesting and engaging of all occupations. . . . Erase from the pages of history the names of soldiers . . . and literature and human life itself would be barren and sterile wastes whereon fancy could not feed, whereon heroism could scarce find a model, loyalty scarce a martyr, liberty not a single victory." Doster would not hold that all virtues evolved from the soldier, but "all except things divine in their nature, things which lay hold of eternal interest, have associated and bound themselves up with the man of war. Whenever we rise in thought above the petty cares of self, whenever the soul goes out in contemplation of the concerns of the human mind, as they have thus far transpired . . . the warrior stalks before the vision and fills the scene." The soldier was noble because war inspired great thoughts and deeds. War and soldiers' blood did more to unite people than did commercial and civil institutions. Only in concluding his speech did Doster turn his attention to the subject of its title and praise the Irish soldiers in American wars: "Literally they have made and preserved this nation."[32]

In defense of Doster's blatant militarism it can be said that he was living in a romantic and sentimental age, a time in which the virtues of nationalism were rarely questioned. Still he took an extreme position even for his own day, and his praise of warfare conflicted with his humanitarian beliefs. In other addresses he stressed the necessity and inevitability of the uniting of mankind; but he also emphasized justice, brotherhood, material betterment, and the role of ideas. In the Strong City oration of 1890, he gave an unqualified endorsement to force and bloodshed. Living in an era of rampant eclecticism, perhaps he saw no contradictions. Disturbing as Doster's utterances may be to modern ears, there were no public objections raised in his time.

Shortly, however, he was to create a statewide sensation. In 1890, the rebellion of the farmers burst on the Kansas political scene. The Republican leadership committed a serious error in the election of that year by making the support of Senator John J. Ingalls' bid for reelection the test of party loyalty. Members of the now powerful Farmers' Alliance were in no mood to vote for candidates for the legislature pledged to Ingalls. To them the senior Senator was a popmpous windbag who had done nothing to alleviate their distress. If nonsupport of Ingalls meant deserting the Republican party, they were prepared to do so.

On July 22, the Marion County Farmers' Alliance and Knights of Labor held their convention. They nominated one of the most well-to-do farmers in the area as their candidate for the state House of Representatives. Leon Riddle recorded that "The convention became very much excited as to whether the candidates for Rep[resentative] should pledge themselves against Jno. J. Ingalls." No pledges were made, "although the convention was evidently anti-Ingalls."[33]

The men of the Alliance were not alone in their antipathy to the Senator. Over his long career he had acquired a host of enemies within the Republican ranks, especially in the "young crowd." These were the rising men of the post-Civil War generation who demanded a greater voice in the party's councils. Ingalls and his ilk had to be pushed aside. Editor Hoch was the archetype of the "young crowd" man. Although he was furious at the Republican managers for making support of Ingalls the *sine qua non* of party allegiance and sympathetic to the Alliance, Hoch and others of his faction refused to leave the established party.[34]

There was yet another group present in the political disturbances of 1890. It included the veteran radicals, the perpetual dissenters who had led the Greenback Anti-Monopoly, and Union Labor parties, among whom Frank Doster was a prominent example. In the revolt of the farmers they saw their opportunity to rise to power in the state. Most of them were town men and professionals—lawyers, editors, doctors, and even some bankers and businessmen. As such they were barred from membership in the Farmers' Alliance. To remedy this they set about organizing a town auxiliary—the Citizens' Alliance. It was reported that Doster went to Topeka in 1890 to help frame a constitution for the Citizens' Alliance. With an organization of their own, the townsmen could identify with the agrarian movement. Their aim was to form a third party—something which the farmers were not at first prepared to do.[35] Many of those who called for the formation of the new party were sincere reformers such as Lorenzo D. Lewelling. Some, however, were professional agitators like Mary Elizabeth Lease. Others were simply old Republican hacks who attached themselves to the movement in the hope of recouping their political fortunes; typical of this group was the notorious James F. Legate of Leavenworth. Finally, there were the enigmas such as Frank Doster. Whether he was motivated by genuine reform impulses or opportunism is a mystery.

In the election of 1890 the Republicans easily won the state offices; but the Alliance men captured a large majority in the House of Representatives. Here they could accomplish their main goal: the unhorsing of "John Jingles." Ingalls' fate was sealed. The question now was, "Who should replace him?" Immediately after the election, the Marion *Times* (quoting the *Rural Kansan*) gave the legislators-elect a suggestion—choose Frank Doster. "There is no man in the state who could and would do more for the farmers in the United States Senate. He is now and has been for the last twelve years, a strong advocate of all economic questions [*sic*] now being advocated by the People's party." Another Republican newspaper in Marion, E. W. Hoch's *Record,* gave Doster's senatorial candidacy its strong endorsement: if a Republican could not have the place, it should go to the most capable man in the opposition and that man, Hoch believed, was his fellow townsman Frank Doster.[36] The Doster boom was not confined to Marion, nor was its impetus simply local pride. Powerful and articulate elements in the new party favored him as Ingalls' replacement. Mary Elizabeth Lease stated publicly that she would refuse to support the front-runners, J. F. Willets and William A. Peffer, "for any position." She was quoted as preferring even Ingalls to either of the other men. "My favorite," said the Kansas Pythoness, "is Judge Frank Doster of Marion, who is, I believe, the brainiest man in the United States to-day, and who is destined to achieve a more than national reputation."[37]

Doster's candidacy was brought to the attention of the legislators by none other than the Judge himself. On December 25, he published an open letter to them, urging the repeal of the "Waiver of Appraisement" statute. By the terms of the law, Doster wrote, a debtor could contract to have his real estate sold in payment for a debt for what it could bring at a sheriff's sale. He also requested legislation which would require courts to postpone a sheriff's sale if the bidding was too low. Doster then offered his services in drafting the bills for these and other judicial reforms. In closing, he aligned himself squarely with the disgruntled farmers:

> I hope this legislature will not be frightened by the clamor and fears of loan agents, that the relief of the people will frighten away capital. My judgment is that capital which desires to come here and live *with us* instead of being frightened away, will prefer to come where people are protected and guaranteed against usurers and extortioners; and as to that capital which merely comes here to live *off of us,* we have had too much already. It is that capital which locates nowhere, and identifies itself with no community but which comes to abide temporarily, while it advantages itself upon the necessities of the people, which is the curse of the industrial world.[38]

Doster's bid for the senate seat failed. The prize went to Peffer, editor of the leading Alliance organ in the state, the *Kansas Farmer*. Beyond sending Peffer to Washington, the Alliance-dominated legislature of 1891 accomplished little. Their inex-

perience was one reason; another was that the Republicans re-
tained the important state elective offices. Thirty-five years
later, an old populist wrote that the Alliance would have fared
better if someone other than the obscure Willets had been the
gubernatorial candidate: "One wonders what might have been
—whether if that convention [of 1890] had put Jerry Simpson
or W. A. Harris or Frank Doster at the head of the ticket, it
might not have pulled a few thousand votes more and had a
greater success."[39]

Although any ambitions Doster may have had for higher
political office were frustrated, it is clear that he was among the
leading figures in the new party. Also, he still held his position
on the bench. Reelection in 1891 could do much to further his
career and the local prestige of the People's party.

On May 14, 1891, he gave what can be considered the opening speech of his campaign. Yet it was more than that—it was
the most important and controversial address of his career. In
it were his central ideas—ideas which he had enunciated before
and would reiterate throughout the remainder of his life. The
address also employed all his usual shock techniques. It became
one of the Populist classics, but not necessarily a classic exposition of Populist dogma. Populism, like any mass movement or
political party, was made up of individuals, men and women of
widely divergent thought and temperament. The oration of May
14 does not illustrate, characterize, or typify the movement; it
can only tell something about one of its more important and
enigmatic leaders.

The occasion was a meeting of the local Farmers' and Citizens' Alliance at the Marion opera house. The Judge had chosen "Mutuality between Capital and Labor" as his topic. He
began by calling his audience's attention to the fact that the
hard times from which they suffered were world-wide, not local.

Thus they need not look for local causes and remedies. Nor were evil conditions elsewhere the result of national or regional injustices. Hardships in Russia were not attributable to her despotic government alone; Ireland did not suffer merely because of landlordism; and France's economic ills could not be blamed solely on her large public debt. Distress was international, and the simple explanations being offered were inadequate.

Some thinkers, however, attempted to probe the more fundamental causes and present new and bold solutions. They were not, Doster reminded his listeners, mere demagogues, cranks, and "calamity shriekers." Rather they were among the most respected members of the academic community and the clergy. The colleges were veritable hotbeds of socialism. William Graham Sumner, Edward Atkinson, David A. Wells, and Francis A. Walker were the "only writers of recognized merit" who continued to adhere to the old theories of economics. The ministry of Episcopal and Unitarian churches "have almost in a body arrayed themselves in favor of a radical change in the laws of social life." Some prominent individual examples were Archbishop Farrar of England and Bishop J. O. S. Huntington in America. Professor Ely of Johns Hopkins was an avowed Christian Socialist and a Bellamyite. "I could call a list of earnest and learned and devout men and women who have arrayed themselves in favor of the masses against the domination of the controlling social forces, that for learning, character, piety and high purpose have never had their superiors in any age of the world; and they are not politicians either. . . . They are in the professor's chair, on the editorial staff, and even in some cases behind the merchant's counter and the banker's desk."

The farmers, said Doster, were only the latest recruits to the movement and the most numerous body within it. They could, however, be congratulated on their leadership: "Ruskin and

Mill and Maurice [William Morris?] in England, Rousseau and Louis Blanc in France, and Karl Marx and a score of others in Germany, and Emerson and Mulford and many other of like character in this country."

Next Doster turned devil's advocate and "defended" the correctness and justice of the established economic system in terms of individual equality, freedom of contract, and the laws of competition and supply and demand. The oppressed had as much "right" to use the same methods and reap the same rewards as did the oppressors. "You know, however, that such answers are insufficient. You know that there is a mockery about them, like unto the gift of a stone when bread is asked, a hollowness and heartlessness which turns the inquirer away with bitterness and despair."

Who then was giving better answers, and what were his solutions? The speaker cited Henry George and his single tax program; Edward Bellamy and "the form of communism, which he styles nationalism"; Count Tolstoy and his belief in manual labor for all; and Malthus and the problem of underproduction. Regardless of the merits of the theories, all had flaws which rendered them unacceptable. And although the Judge was heartily in favor of currency expansion, government loans, and lower tariffs, these proposals were also mere "palliatives and stimulants, temporary and spasmodic in their effect. They proceed upon no just conception of the disease which afflicts the body politic. . . . You cannot found and defend a philosophy upon the relative cost of a couple of pairs of breeches purchased under high and low tariff."

Doster then turned to the main body of the address: an analysis of, but not a solution for, the wrongs of the prevailing system. The essence of his theory was that the times were out of joint because there was a misconception of the relationship between capital and labor. To say that the correct relationship between the two was mutuality was "asinine gibberish." There could be no mutuality without an equality of interest in what was produced; and no such equality existed. Capital was simply ownership, and the object of production was not ownership but use. Labor, moreover, had created capital and the sole function of capital (or ownership) was to be a trustee for labor which, according to Doster's thinking, was synonymous with use.

Departing from his cold and often confusing abstractions, Doster described the "fruits of the opposing theory":

> An accursed strife by everybody for the ownership of something which another must use, so that out of the tribute for its use idleness and ease may be enjoyed. For ownership[,] the sordid[,] avaricious clutcher after other men's homes absorbs the common heritage of us all, and withholds it except upon terms of abject and remorseless tenancy. For ownership the great railways and navigation lines seize upon the public franchises, and dole out their use to the necessitous traveler and shipper at profits, which in half a century have made the transportation business the greatest capitalistic institution of any age. For ownership the money usurer gathers in from the avenue of trade, and the ways of industry, the circulating medium of the realm, and burns up much that the balance may be more sought after, and then buries it, out of sight, until Antonio will pledge a pound of flesh, nearest the heart, for three months use of it.

Having related his theorizing to concrete terms readily understandable to his h e a r e r s—tenancy, freight rates, tight money, and high interest rates—he went on to explain that

> Stripped to its nakedness the proposition is that the owner of property does not possess with respect to such property an equality of right with the user of it, and upon the truth of that proposition, let me say to you, members of the Farmer's and Citizen's Alliance, and you People's party men, rests

the entire fabric of your political platforms and your demand for industrial reform. . . . You demand that the lenders of money, the owners of that species of capital, scale down their interest rates to accommodate you as the users of the same. Do you not? You demand that pools and trusts be prohibited, because you as the users of the property they sell, have greater interests in the same than they as owners have. Do you not? You demand a repeal or modification of the patent and copyright laws, because you as the user of a machine or the reader of a book have greater rights in the same than the inventor or author has. Do you not? And you are right in all these things.

Thus, Doster argued, the audience was in agreement with the theory which they had at first thought to be "revolutionary and untenable." They declared their repudiation of the "dogma of mutuality between labor and capital, or between owner and user, and . . . asserted that the rights of the user of a thing were paramount to the rights of its owner."

The Judge contended that the technological revolution of the past few decades had made necessary the "immediate and unconditional application [of the principle of the paramount rights of the user] to the affairs of men." Until recent years there had been a relatively simple economy; villages and even farms had been self-sufficient; men owned thir own tools and produced for themselves. Denying that he was characterizing former conditions as the "good old times," or that he regretted their passing, he wished only to assert that the new industrial age demanded a different social and economic system; one which recognized the rights of the user in a complex and interdependent society.

You can't have, each of you, your own agricultural implement factory, your private railroad and telegraph line, your warehouse and elevator, your national bank of which you are the sole stock-holder, your shoe and clothing manufactories, but you must be content to let all these institutions, the capital in which and the product of which you use pass into that form of interest termed ownership, and be operated for profit to the owner, and not benefit to the user.

Doster closed by saying that he had not tried to point out the means by which the subordination of the interests of capital to those of labor could be effected. He would do that "at such opportunity as hereafter presents itself."[40]

For the detached reader of today, Frank Doster's opera house address of 1891 is an innocuous document. Little in it would seem radical in light of modern economic thought; his sentiments were not essentially at variance with the prevailing ideas of his own day. Had not Carnegie applied the Calvinist concept of trusteeship to modern capitalism? Had not Adam Smith's teachings made the labor theory of value an article of the capitalistic faith? In 1861 Lincoln said in three succinct sentences all that Doster tried to explain in an hour's speech: "Labor is prior to, and independent of, capital. Capital is only the fruit of labor, and never could have existed if labor had not first existed. Labor is the superior of capital, and deserves much the higher consideration."[41] Doster himself had gone to some pains to point out that respected clergymen and academicians and many polite journals were espousing the same views. He could also have explained, as he later did, that much of his thinking was based on common-law principles expounded by Sir Matthew Hale and more recently by Chief Justice Waite.

Yet Republicans and Alliance members alike accepted the oration as a declaration of radicalism and the speaker was largely responsible for this interpretation. Rather than cite Waite and Hale, he led his listeners to believe that his ideas stemmed from Louis Blanc, Rousseau, and Karl Marx. He emphasized repeatedly that his views were "radical," "peculiar," "probably obnoxious," "unpopular," and "at variance with the thought of the age, and all ages in fact." Both sympathetic and hostile listeners accepted him at his word. The address was subsequently known as Judge Doster's "socialistic speech."

Inflammatory language alone cannot account for the sensation brought on by the address. It was an election year and the Judge was seeking another term. In 1887 the Republicans of the Twenty-fifth Judicial District could afford to support an independent candidate. In 1891 a new political force was challenging their monopoly. Defeating Frank Doster was tantamount to defeating Populism in that portion of central Kansas. The Populists likewise viewed the election as a test of their strength; their man Doster had to be returned to the bench.

The first adverse response to Doster's address was a mild letter to the *Record* from W. W. Runyon, a Marion school teacher. He referred to the writings of Goethe and Ibsen to argue that social reform must be accomplished largely by individuals and not governmental institutions as Doster had suggested. A second letter from Runyon ("Public Evils and Proposed Remedies: Thoughts Called Out by Judge Doster's Address") was more critical. He charged that Doster's thinking was in opposition to three of the Ten Commandments: the commandment to love one's neighbor and the injunctions against stealing and coveting a neighbor's possessions. Runyon's third letter ("Further Thoughts") was still stronger. The Judge was a "special pleader" and unworthy of being on the bench. A clergyman, Elder H. A. Kerr, wrote that while Doster's socialism was of the more humane variety, as opposed to the "base" and "vicious" radicalism of Johann Most, the Judge was too much the visionary.[42]

A letter from "Farmer" in the Marion *Times* took Doster to

task in a less sophisticated manner: "Judge Doster says that the user of a thing has greater rights to it than its owner. He tells us farmers that! We didn't laugh when he said it, but some of us have laughed since. I raise a crop of wheat and am the owner of it, I suppose. I can use a part of it. But other folks have a better right to it than I have! Jerusha!"[43]

The *Times* had its fun with the following "Scene at the Breakfast Table."

> Child—Pa, please tell me what Dosterism is.
> Father—You can't understand it child. I don't understand it very well myself.
> Child—But do tell me what it is, pa, please; that's a good daddy.
> Father—Oh well then, it is this; the user's rights is better than the owner's, or something like that.
> Child—Does that mean, pa, that I may visit Mr. Doster's pear-orchard and help my ———?
> Father—No you naughty boy. It means —— be still and drink your milk.[44]

Doster's pronouncement had gained such currency in the area that a local business establishment could announce that

> "THE USERS RIGHTS MAY BE PARAMOUNT TO THE OWNERS"
> But the place to get fresh bread, cakes, pies and a fancy line of confectioneries, ice cream and cool summer drinks is at the 'Excelsior Bakery.' . . .[45]

Edward W. Hoch's initial reaction to the speech was calm enough. Confesing that he had missed the Judge's opening remarks, he wrote that: "Mr. Doster is an entertaining speaker, and it is always a pleasure to listen to him, but so far as we could catch the trend of his thought we are not prepared to endorse the ideas he advanced." Perhaps the death of Doster's mother shortly after the delivering of the address kept Hoch from writing a strong attack at the time; in the following month, however, he challenged Doster's opinions. After praising the literary quality of the speech, Hoch went on to deny the absence of mutuality between labor and capital. Legislation for the regulation of corporations was evidence of mutuality, not antagonism, between the two. Hoch also saw "atheism" in Doster's statement that the "only law which the user of capital is bound to observe is that law which finds its end and sanction in himself—the law of self interest." Finally, the *Record* editor scolded the local Alliance leaders for endorsing Doster's sentiments.[46]

The July 17 *Record* printed an exchange between the editor and the Judge. Doster wrote that the most accurate term for the relationship between labor and capital was "reciprocity," not mutuality; for mutuality implied equality and the relationship was not equal since labor (or the user) had greater rights. Hoch replied with an elaboration of his views. Doster responded by pointing out that Hoch had recognized the superior rights of the user by introducing a bill in the 1889 legislature designed to deprive "Lord" Scully and other alien landholders of their Kansas lands. Finally the Judge denied that he had advocated socialism; rather he had laid down the moral and ethical bases of social and economic relationships. In the next issue Hoch wrote that Doster's theories originated in the Garden of Eden where the Devil told Adam and Eve to take the apple because the rights of the user were paramount to those of the owner.

Doster's address made him the darling of the local Populists. At the Labor Day celebration for which he delivered the main speech, there were several banners proclaiming "The Rights of the user are paramount to the owner's" and "No more receivers over crops—Doster." Two weeks later the county People's party convention (for which Leon Riddle was secretary) resolved "That we endorse the Judge's address as a clear exhibit, portrayal and able defense of the great foundation stone upon which our party and its platform are founded.[47]

The Republicans of Marion County were in sympathy with the demands of the angry farmers. They had no quarrel with the major tenets of the Alliance–Populist program. In their August convention they passed a resolution favoring free coinage of silver; they denounced railroad rate discrimination and fraudulent securities issues.[48] Still they faced the task of downing a challenge to their supremacy. To do so they could not assault Populist principles; but they could attack individual candidates. Judge Doster's alleged socialism made him particularly vulnerable. The Republicans accordingly threw the full weight of their oratory and editorializing against him. Other Populist candidates were virtually ignored.

In August the Republican Central Committee for the Twenty-fifth Judicial District called for a "tripartisan" convention to select an opponent for Doster, who had by his statements, they announced, shown himself to be out of sympathy with the laws he had to interpret, i. e., property rights. A convention of eighteen delegates from each of the three counties met the following month. Lucien Earle, a McPherson Democrat, was unanimously endorsed by the "Anti-Socialistic Judicial Convention."[49]

The nominee then published an announcement to the people of the district: "In response to the solicitations of a large number of people of Marion, McPherson and Chase counties, who believe that the Judiciary is the 'sheet anchor' of our liberties and the 'balance wheel' of American institutions, and that the office of Judge should be free and untrammeled and in no way connected with partizan politics, I announce myself as a candidate for the office of judge of this . . . district."[50]

Earle had been one of six Democratic lawyers in his county to endorse Doster in 1887. Editor Hoch, one of the Marion County delegates to the "Anti-Socialistic" gathering had also been his champion that year. He now had to justify his previous endorsement. He had urged Doster's appointment, said Hoch, because he had the backing of the district bar and no Republican wanted the job; he had supported his bid for a full term because he thought Doster deserved one. But now the Judge "had confirmed in unmistakable language, the rumors which had been afloat here for years concerning his unsoundness on social and governmental problems." Editor J. C. Fast of the *Anzeiger* also repudiated Doster. He warned his fellow Mennonites that "Socialism is totally contrary to the statutes of our form of government, is contrary to religion and is therewith a spirit out of the abyss, which threatens us with misery and corruption. No Christian voter should support this element in any way, in order not to make himself a participant in the sins (of others)."[51]

Doster struck back at his detractors, particularly his former supporters of the press and bar. He lashed out at the "corrupt" and "venal" press of the district, giving as examples Hoch's *Record* and the Marion *Times*. The newspapermen responded in kind, as did the members of the bar, after Doster accused his colleagues of "pinheadism."[52]

The most serious incident of the campaign was an altercation between Doster and one of his fellow lawyers. James S. Dean, a young Marion attorney, accused the Judge of forgery and falsifying evidence in a case in which Dean was interested. When Doster heard of it, he sought out Dean on the streets of Marion. The furious Judge accosted him, brandished a pistol, and demanded to know if the younger man had made the charges. When Dean replied affirmatively, Doster threatened to "shoot his damn heart out." Dean informed him that he was unarmed, whereupon Doster told him to get a weapon. Fortunately, bystanders intervened and separated the two. Doster apologized publicly for the incident; but the opposition was quick to point out that the act was evidence of his ungovernable temper.[53]

The judicial contest in the Twenty-fifth District had attracted state-wide attention by the close of the campaign. Democrats as well as Republicans hoped for the defeat of the Marion "socialist." The Kansas City *Times* commented that "Mr. Earle's election is becoming more assured as the real meaning of Doster's heresies is understood." Late in October a leading Democrat, the able and respected David Overmeyer of Topeka, came to Strong City to combat the radical Judge's principles. Socialism, Overmeyer told his audience, was clearly not the solution to the problems of Kansas. The true remedy was a return to Jeffersonian doctrines, because the present ills —demonetization of silver, corporate larceny, and the rape of the public lands—were the results of too much government. Surely the socialistic schemes of Judge Doster and his ilk would bring more governmental oppression. Socialism, moreover, needed coercion. Authoritarian Sparta was a success; the benevolent systems of Fourier and Owen failed.[54]

In the November election, Lucien Earle emerged victorious over his now famous rival. The defeat of the incumbent was decisive, with Earle winning 4,939 votes to Doster's 4,234 and gaining a majority in all three counties. "Judge Earle, that sounds good," crowed W. A. Morgan. Outside the district some observers registered surprise at Doster's defeat, for many believed him to have been invincible in his bailiwick. A number of reasons could be advanced to explain the failure to be reelected: the hostility of the majority of the district's editors and lawyers; the "socialistic" speech; the opposition of the Mennonites; and the pistol-drawing affair. Perhaps a more fundamental cause was that it was simply a bad year for Populism. Defeat was general throughout the state. In 1890 the Populists had won 324 local offices in Kansas as opposed to 71 for the Republicans. This time the Republicans were victorious in 277 contests while the People's party won only 127. In Marion County the Republicans swept all the county offices.[55]

The Republicans were, of course, ecstatic. And at least some leaders of the Alliance in Kansas were not displeased. In a cryptic article, the *Kansas Farmer* (perhaps with reference to Doster) declared that the Alliance and the People's party were independent entities and that the election had brought a "beneficent effect on the Alliance organization, ridding it of an element that was calculated to breed discord and leaving it absolutely free from political entanglements."[56]

Contrary to Republican hopes and predictions, however, the movement was far from dead; nor had they heard the last of Frank Doster. The address of May 14 may have been a factor in his defeat, but it made him the idol of the Populists in his own area and he was acknowledged as "the Daniel Webster of the Populist party in Kansas."[57]

NOTES

[1]C. S. Burch, *Hand-Book of Marion County* (Chicago: C. S. Burch, 1888); *Cottonwood Valley Times,* July 4, 1889.

[2]L. H. Riddle, MS Diary, 1887–1891, microfilm copy at Kansas State Historical Society, entries of Dec. 23, 1888, and Oct. 10, 1887; "Marion Town Co. 1st Addition to Marion," A. E. Case MSs, University of Kansas Library; *Doster* v. *Sterling,* 33 Kan. 381 (1885); *Doster* v. *Beebe,* 36 Kan. 666 (1887).

[3]James C. Malin, *A Concern about Humanity: Notes on Reform, 1872–1912, at the National and Kansas Levels of Thought* (Lawrence, Kansas: The Author, 1964), p. 139.

[4]*Cottonwood Valley Times,* June 9, 1887, and June 23, 1887.

[5]Riddle Diary, entries for May 16, 1887, and Sept. 19, 1888; Marion *Record,* Aug. 29, 1884.

[6]James C. Malin, *Winter Wheat in the Golden Belt of Kansas: A Study in Adaptation to Subhumid Geographical Environment* (Lawrence, Kansas: University of Kansas Press, 1944), pp. 248–49.

[7]Riddle Diary, entries of Nov. 10, 1889, and May 18, 1890.

[8]*Ibid.,* entry of Sept. 4, 1888.

[9]Homer E. Socolofsky, "The Scully Land System in Marion County," *Kansas Historical Quarterly,* XVIII (Nov., 1950), 337–75.

[10]*Cottonwood Valley Times,* Nov. 22, 1888.

[11]This and other correspondence cited below regarding the appointment are found in Governors' Correspondence, John A. Martin, "Applications, Endorsements and Remonstrances," Archives Division, Kansas State Historical Society.

[12]John E. Harper to Martin, March 9, 1887; John and Dennis Madden, March 9, 1887; L. Houk to Martin, March 11, 1887; L. B. Kellogg to Martin, March 18, 1887 (see note 11).

[13]Grisham to A. B. Campbell, March 12, 1887 (see note 11).

[14]C. E. Hait to Martin, March 14, 1887; Kelly to Martin, March 15, 1887 (see note 11).

[15]C. F. Brooker, *et al.,* to Martin, March 14, 1887 (see note 11).

[16]J. Ware Butterfield to Martin, March 14, 1887 (see note 11).

[17]Kirke Mechem (ed.), *Annals of Kansas, 1886–1925* (Topeka: Kansas State Historical Society, 1954–56), I, 34.

[18]*Minutes of the Fourth Annual Session of the Bar Association of the State of Kansas* (Topeka: 1887), pp. 57–58.

[19]*Ibid.,* p. 58.

[20]*Chase County Leader,* May 12, 1887.

[21]Marion *Record,* Aug. 19, 1887; *Chase County Leader,* Aug. 25, 1887.

[22]Lincolnville *Star,* Sept. 3, 1887; *Chase County Leader,* Sept. 1, 1887.

[23]*Cottonwood Valley Times,* Sept. 8, 1887; Marion *Record,* Sept. 9, 1887.

[24]*Marion County Anzeiger,* Sept. 9, 1887; *Cottonwood Valley Times,* Nov. 3, 1887.

[25]*Ibid.,* Sept. 22, 1887; *Chase County Leader,* Sept. 22, 1887.

[26]Riddle Diary, entries of Oct. 24, Oct. 31, Nov. 3, Nov. 4, Nov. 7, and Nov. 8, 1887.

[27]*Ibid.,* entry of Nov. 9, 1887; Secretary of State of the State of Kansas, *Sixth Biennial Report* (Topeka: 1888), p. 76; *Cottonwood Valley Times,* Nov. 7, 1887.

[28]Marion *Record,* April 13, 1888; *Cottonwood Valley Times,* May 17, 1888.

[29]Riddle Diary, entry of May 30, 1890.

[30]Malin, *A Concern about Humanity,* pp. 140–42; Malin, *Confounded Rot about Napoleon: Reflections upon Science and Technology, Nationalism, World Depression of the Eighteen-Nineties, and Afterwards* (Lawrence, Kansas: The Author, 1961), pp. 205–06.

[31]Marion *Record,* June 6, 1890.

[32]Malin, *A Concern about Humanity,* pp. 140–42.

[33]Riddle Diary, entry of July 22, 1890.

[34]Michael J. Brodhead, "The Early Career of E. W. Hoch, 1870–1904" (unpublished Master's thesis, University of Kansas, 1962), pp. 48–49.

[35]Malin, *A Concern about Humanity,* p. 38.

[36]Marion *Times,* Nov. 20, 1890; Marion *Record,* Jan. 16, 1891.

[37]Marion *Times,* Jan. 8, 1891.

[38]*Ibid.,* Dec. 25, 1890.

[39]W. P. Harrington, "The Populist Party in Kansas," *Kansas Historical Collections,* XVI (1923–1925), 413.

[40]The full text of the speech is found in the May 29, 1891, *Central Advocate* (Marion).

[41]Roy P. Basler (ed.), *The Collected Works of Abraham Lincoln* (New Brunswick, N. J.: Ruters University Press, 1953) V, 52.

[42]Marion *Record,* June 5, 12, 19, and 26, 1891.

[43]*Ibid.,* July 9, 1891.

[44]Marion *Times,* Oct. 1, 1891.

[45]*Ibid.*

[46]Marion *Record,* May 22, June 19, and July 10, 1891.

[47]Marion *Times,* Sept. 3, 1891; Marion *Record,* Sept. 18, 1891.

[48]Marion *Times,* Aug. 20, 1891.

[49]Marion *Record,* Aug. 21, 1891; *Ibid.,* Sept. 18, 1891.

[50]*Chase County Leader,* Sept. 24, 1891.

[51]Marion *Record,* Sept. 18, 1891; Hillsboro *Anzeiger,* Oct. 9, 1891. The author acknowledges the help of John G. Gagliardo in translating passages from the *Anzeiger.*

[52]Malin, *A Concern about Humanity,* p. 147; Marion *Record,* Oct. 30, 1891.

[53]Marion *Record,* Oct. 30, 1891; *Chase County Leader,* Oct. 29, 1891; *Kansas Democrat* (Topeka), Oct. 30, 1891; Marion *Times,* Oct. 29 and Nov. 19, 1891.

[54]Kansas City *Times,* Oct. 23, 1891.

[55]Secretary of State of the State of Kansas, *Eighth Biennial Report* (Topeka: 1892), p. 89; *Chase County Leader,* Nov. 5, 1891; *Weekly Record* (Lawrence), Nov. 6, 1891; Raymond C. Miller, " The Populist Party in Kansas" (unpublished Ph.D. thesis, University of Chicago, 1928), p. 213; Marion *Record,* Nov. 6, 1891.

[56]*Kansas Farmer,* Nov. 11, 1891.

[57]Kansas City *Star,* Nov. 29, 1896.

3

NO GREATER DISASTER
COULD COME TO KANSAS

A S THE Kansas Populists launched their 1892 campaign, Frank Doster emerged as one of the party's major intellectuals. Cold as he was in person, his speechmaking and writing gained a devoted statewide following for him.

In the campaigns of the early 1890's, the emphasis of his addresses and articles was on the nature and purpose of government. He voiced his thoughts on two levels. On the one hand, he spread his gospel of governmental action on the stump using easily understood Populist rhetoric. In August of 1892 at Fredonia he was reported to have cried: "You must believe in paternalism, socialism or if you like to call it anarchism, and if you don't believe in the sub-treasury scheme you are no people's party man."[1]

Doster was capable of expressing himself in a more polished manner than what the Republicans called "calamity howling." In the October issue of the Kansas literary periodical *The Agora* he addressed himself to the topic "What Government is For." The article was an erudite blending of the ideas of Elisha Mulford, Marx, Herbert Spencer, and John Fiske. He told his readers that political thinkers in the past had too often considered only the origin and form of government. Such inquiries made government an abstraction without justification or purpose—"an antagonistic and overawing personality, self-existent, self-conscious, self-sufficient, and undying, with a life and purpose of its own as distinguished from its people, either individually or collectively."[2] Government was an organic institution and, like any organism, it underwent evolution. No longer should men consider it a tyrant; nor should they think of it merely as the guarantor of political rights. Society too had evolved from the barbarism of clan and tribal organizations. Each step in the process brought men closer together, bringing greater harmony and less social friction. The concept of government had to keep pace with new social forms. Now that is was generally recognized that sovereign power was vested in the people, they should use political institutions for the ultimate, obvious, and inevitable goal of government, which was "no other than the equality of human brotherhood."[3]

Government, Doster wrote, was destined to concern itself with "the regulation of its subjects in their immediate personal and business relations." He denied that government "has its ground-work in the passing fact of commercial strife," because political institutions could not be based permanently on the greed and selfishness of men. Government was not merely to provide "security for material accumulations." Rather it was to be used to promote solidarity and equality by preventing its subjects from following their selfish impulses.[4]

As he so often did, Doster admitted that his views were "radically divergent" from those of most men. But "to the ignorant, unable to comprehend an universal law of life, and to the vicious, who, comprehending, yet rebel against its gracious sway, it may be said that truth cannot be outblown by a clamor of dissent, or stigmatized into silence by odium and reproach." And, lest timid souls be "startled by the prophecy of that ultimate solidarity of humanity, which leaves no room for the play of individual action to individual ends," Doster left his readers with the "reassuring words" of William Cullen Bryant:

> Gently, so have good men taught,
> Gently and without pain, the old shall glide
> Into the new; The eternal flow of things,
> Like a bright river of the fields of Heaven,
> Shall journey onward in perpetual peace.[5]

Earlier that year he advocated a type of governmental activity which was repugnant to many Kansans. He had supported a plan for state-owned liquor stores. Once again he drew the fire of E. W. Hoch, a staunch supporter of prohibition. To Hoch it was further evidence of Doster's "socialism." As the 1892 campaign reached a climax, the Marion editor wrote a long letter to the Topeka *Capital* denouncing Doster as a disciple of Rousseau, Marx, and Louis Blanc.[6]

The fulminations of Hoch and other Republicans were in vain. The People's party emerged victorious in the November elections, winning all the state elective offices, a seat in the state Supreme Court, and a majority in the upper house of the legislature. Although not a candidate for any office, Doster was prominent in the campaign and shared in the glories of victory. A northern Kansas farmer recorded in his diary that "Judge Doster spoke Saturday evening in Concordia[;] the P[eople's] P[arty] Ratification was an immense affair. The court house was packed with people. The speech was well received by the people." After the inaugural in Topeka, a huge crowd met in Representative Hall for a Populist love feast. Doster was among those addressing the joyous "Pops." Others giving speeches were party luminaries Mary E. Lease, Jerry Simpson, Rev. W. G. Todd, Annie L. Diggs, Justice Stephen Allen, and G. C. Clemens.[7]

The Populists, however, had scant cause for celebrating. The failure to win a majority in the lower house caused the Lewelling administration two years of grief and a record barren of substantial gains. The Populists could claim only fifty-eight representatives holding certificates of election, but the Republican members of the House held sixty-three. Among the Republican representatives was Doster's antagonist E. W. Hoch, who had based his campaign largely on attacks against his radical fellow townsman. There were, according to the Populists, enough Republicans whose elections were questionable to challenge the old party's claim to a clear majority. In many of the counties there had been irregularities which they claimed had cost the People's party candidates a number of victories. In one of the contested elections Doster, W. C. Webb, and G. C. Clemens acted as attorneys for Joseph Rosenthal, Democrat of Haskell County. When the case was taken to the state Supreme Court, it was ruled that the House itself should judge whether the plaintiff was entitled to a seat.[8]

On the opening day of the legislative session, January 10, the Republicans refused to recognize the Populist Secretary of State as the temporary presiding officer, since his list of members did not include those Republicans whose elections were questioned. Bedlam broke loose when both parties proceeded to elect their own officers. The result was two Houses of Representatives, each claiming to have a majority. The Republicans selected George Douglass as Speaker and Hoch as Speaker pro tempore; J. M. Dunsmore was elected as the Speaker of the Populist House. Both sides refused to vacate the hall and the result was an all-night session.

A committee composed of the state chairmen of all three parties and other prominent figures, among them Jerry Simpson and Doster, met in an effort to break the deadlock. They drafted an agreement which called for a one-day adjournment; all members and would-be members could return to the hall the following day. Both Houses ratified this preliminary compromise and ended the twenty-six-hour session. Doster had presented a lengthy, legalistic compromise plan which would have allowed the state Supreme Court to settle the question. When it was not accepted by the committee, he walked out. The Republican press charged Doster and Simpson with interfering with the peace negotiations and with ignoring the wishes of the Populist legislators. Doster, Simpson, and Populist chairman John Briedenthal were each accused of being guided solely by personal ambition and the desire to be the next United States senator from Kansas.[9]

In the eyes of the Republicans, Doster was fast becoming the evil genius behind the turmoil. Businessman J. Ware Butterfield of Marion County wrote a letter from Topeka to the Marion *Record* describing Doster as the leading attorney and advisor to the Dunsmore House. Republican Speaker Douglass later declared that the Populists had "got Doster's brain to working and after sitting in a room four nights with ice on his head, he said if any man thought he ought to be in the legislature he could go into it and draw pay until the majority voted him out." When Governor Lewelling recognized the Populist House, the Topeka *Capital* blamed Doster, Simpson, and Briedenthal for pressuring him into the act. The Democratic Kansas City *Times* accused Doster, Lewelling, and Simpson of trying to set up a commune "on the ruins of the social organization of the State." The opposition press generally referred to Doster as the "assistant Governor."[10]

While the dispute between the Houses raged, the time arrived for selecting a United States senator. The Republicans had seventy-nine votes in the Senate and House, the Democrats five, and the Populists eighty-one. Had the Populists allowed their "fiat" members (those without certificates and claiming seats) to vote they would have had more than the eighty-three votes necessary to elect. The party leadership, however, feared that if the "fiat" members voted, the man chosen for senator would not be seated in Washington. Also, many believed that by electing a Democrat, the five Democratic members who held the balance of power would support the claim of the Dunsmore House to legitimacy.

The front-runner among the Democratic possibilities was John Martin of Junction City. Many Populists (Mary E. Lease being the most vocal) were opposed to such bargaining and demanded that one of their own be selected. The major contenders among the Populists were Doster, Briedenthal, and former Governor Charles Robinson. Doster was the favorite of Mrs. Lease and several other leaders. His chances were believed to have become greater after the three Democratic representatives voted to recognize the Douglass House.[11]

On the evening of January 23, the Populist legislators caucused in an effort to select a senatorial nominee. They were badly split, with the "middle-of-the-road" element determined to block Martin. Martin led on the first ballot with thirty-four votes, but fifty members refused to support any Democrat and divided their votes among sixteen "straight-out" candidates. After four hours and nine ballots, Martin had thirty-five votes, Doster twenty-seven, and Briedenthal seventeen. At this point the Martin men, fearing he would lose after more balloting, secured an adjournment.[12]

The following day the Senate and the Douglass and Dunsmore houses met in joint session to choose a senator. The Republicans were solidly for Joseph W. Ady. The Populists were still far from unity. The combined vote was Ady seventy-seven,

Briedenthal twenty-five, Doster twenty-four, and Martin fifteen.[13]

The Populists then called a second caucus in the Senate chamber. After thirteen ballots the minor candidates had dropped out, and on the fourteenth ballot Briedenthal withdrew. The contest was now between Martin and Doster. The result depended on the last of the Briedenthal supporters. Had four of them joined the Doster forces, victory would have been his; but only three did so, leaving Doster with forty-three votes to Martin's forty-four. Angry "straight-outs" demanded a recount. Then a wrangle followed over making the nomination unanimous, which resulted in a motion requiring both men to appear before the caucus to speak.

By one-thirty in the morning, Doster and Martin arrived. Martin made what was described as a "pathetic appeal" for the nomination in which he endorsed the People's party platform except for the subtreasury plan. After a brief talk by Doster, the caucus, at three o'clock, balloted once again. The outcome was forty-nine for Martin and thirty-five for Doster. There was still too much resentment to make the nomination unanimous, and no attempt was made. On January 25, the joint session of the Legislature reconvened and elected Martin as the new Kansas senator. One adamant "Pop" cast his ballot for Doster, but Doster, who was present, persuaded him to withdraw the vote.[14]

Well might the Marion Populist have harbored a bitter resentment at his defeat by a Democrat. As in all his political setbacks, however, he expressed no anger or disappointment. Although his middle-of-the-road supporters remained dissatisfied, many Populists were not displeased with the outcome. General James B. Weaver, the party's 1892 presidential nominee, believed that the selection of Martin, who was in sympathy with most of the Populist demands, was "the very best possible result." Weaver hoped, however, that Martin would be "the last so-called Democrat elected by Populist votes." The *Kansas Farmer* expressed itself as "entirely satisfied" with Martin's election.[15]

Meanwhile the dispute continued between the two bodies claiming to be the true House of Representatives. The Douglass and Dunsmore houses met and carried on legislative business in the same hall. Finally, on February 14, the Republicans, on the motion of E. W. Hoch, voted to arrest Ben Rich, clerk of the Dunsmore House, for "interrupting" the proceedings of the House by "loud and boisterous language and unlawful noises": that is, for calling the roll of the Dunsmore House.[16] When the Republican officials attempted to arrest Rich a struggle ensued, whereupon Governor Lewelling called on the Sheriff of Shawnee County for assistance. The Sheriff, a Republican, refused.

On the following day the Populist members assembled in Represenative Hall and locked the doors. The Republicans, finding themselves barred from the Hall, regrouped at the Copeland Hotel. There they secured a sledge-hammer and marched back to the capitol, led by Representatives Hoch and J. A. Cubbison. They battered down the door, rushed triumphantly into the chamber, and dispersed the Populists.

Again the Governor called upon a Republican to restore order, this time Colonel J. W. F. Hughes of the Third Regiment of the Kansas National Guard. When Hughes refused, Lewelling dismissed him from the state's service. The Governor then called eight National Guard companies, a battery of light artillery, and a Gatling gun unit to active duty. For several days the militiamen patrolled the capitol grounds and legislative halls. When some of them tried to remove a Republican journalist from the House galleries, he announced that he had every right to occupy a seat there because his right as a user was paramount to that of the owners. The Populist representatives were reported to have replied "Judge Doster be damned," and the reporter was ejected forcibly.[17]

Republicans were convinced that Doster was largely responsible for the chaotic state of affairs. A delegation of Republicans, believing that Lewelling was receptive to a compromise, called on the Governor. When they arrived in the Governor's chambers, they found the Marion radical there also. After hearing their proposal, Lewelling told them that he wished to consult with Doster before making a decision. Following a brief discussion with him, the Governor told the Republicans that their plan was unsatisfactory. In its report on the meeting the Topeka *Capital* declared: "It is plain to everyone who has been around the executive office that Doster is running Lewelling, and that every move has been made on Doster's advice. It is plain too, that but for the interference of Doster the trouble would have been settled long ago. Doster has urged all the revolutionary measures and the advice of more conservative members of the party has not been heeded."[18]

As the situation grew more desperate, Lewelling and the Republicans moved toward compromise. They agreed to follow the state Supreme Court's decision in a pending case which, in essence, would determine whether the Douglass or Dunsmore House was the true House of Representatives in Kansas. An employee of the Missouri Pacific, L. C. Gunn, had been summoned before the committee on elections of the Douglass House which was investigating irregularities in the Labette County election of 1892. He refused to testify on the grounds that the Republican House was not the legitimate

House, and was arrested. Gunn then sought a writ of habeas corpus from the state Supreme Court.

By allowing the matter to be settled by the court, the Populists placed themselves at a disadvantage. Two of the three justices, Horton and Johnston, were Republicans. Only newly elected Stephen Allen was a Populist. The Republicans, moreover, selected some of the best legal talent from the Republican and Democratic parties to represent respondent C. C. Clevenger, sergeant-at-arms of the Douglass House: Chester I. Long (later a United States senator), T. C. Garver, W. H. Rossington, David Overmeyer, and D. C. Tillotson. The Lewelling administration began selecting outstanding Populist lawyers to oppose them. Attorney General John L. Little wrote to the Governor asking him to "employ as my assistants such counsel as you shall deem proper" in order to "protect the interests of the State." Lewelling accordingly pressed Frank Doster, G. C. Clemens, and W. C. Webb into service.[19]

At the trial Webb and Doster were active in examining most of the witnesses for the state. Doster also delivered the major summation for the Populist side. In a long and, according to the Republican press, tedious speech of one hour and nineteen minutes, the Populist attorney reviewed the election irregularities in the various counties and denied the right of the court to interfere with a legislative body. He also contended that the recognition extended to the Dunsmore House by the Senate and the Governor made it the *de jure* House of Representatives.[20]

The court's decision, perhaps predictably, followed political lines. Horton and Johnston held that the Supreme Court had the right to decide upon the case since it had original jurisdiction in habeas corpus cases. They further held that a certificate of election to the legislature was prima facie evidence of membership, and persons holding them were entitled to participate in the organizing of the House and to vote for its officers until it was proven that they were not legally elected members. Justice Allen followed Doster's reasoning in his dissent. Allen wrote that the court had "no jurisdiction to decide political questions" and that those holding certificates but whose seats were contested were not eligible to vote for House officers.[21]

The Gunn decision was handed down on February 25 and the Populist legislators, in accordance with the previous agreement, returned, *sans* "fiat" members, to the Hall and recognized the Douglass House. The issue, however, was far from dead. The Republicans could make political capital of the Populist-inspired "anarchy" and the Populists were anxious to prove that they were in the right. *The Agora* devoted much of its April issue to a symposium entitled "The Late Conflict." Edward Hoch and Charles S. Gleed presented the Republican arguments and Doster and Clemens were the Populist apologists. Hoch blamed the entire affair on the pernicious advice given to Lewelling by "assistant Governor" Doster, Clemens ("the Topeka Anarchist"), the "coarse" James F. Legate, and Judge W. C. Webb. It was these "anarchists" and "socialists" who had convinced the Governor that "the mathematical difficulty of making fifty-eight exceed sixty-four" could be surmounted. Clemens' article was a witty piece emphasizing the comic-opera elements of the war. He ended it, however, by accusing the sheriff of Shawnee County of treason. Gleed wrote an able statement on "What the Farmers have Netted." He charged that there were no true representatives of the agricultural intrests in the Governor's closest circle. Webb, Doster, and Clemens were "no more in tune with the farmers of Kansas than with the Salvation Army." Doster's analysis ("What

It was About") was largely a review of the election irregularities and a reiteration of his arguments before the Supreme Court.[22]

The continuing debate was not confined to the polite journals. Joseph K. Hudson, editor of the Topeka *Capital,* published a series of *Letters to Governor Lewelling* during and after the "war." He accused the Governor of plotting to impeach Chief Justice Horton and replace him with Doster: "Doster the anarchist will dishonor the seat so long honored by Judge Horton." Hudson described the administration as "created by Bellamyism, nursed by the principles of Doster and Herr Most and made ridiculous by Simpson and Willets." In one of the "letters" he declared that Lewelling's efforts to have Doster elected United States senator were "a fitting tribute from the head of the present rebellion against the constitutional authority of the House to the most outspoken and sincere anarchist in your variegated combine." Ed Hoch wrote a pamphlet on *The Last War* which was distributed from the state Republican headquarters. He singled out Doster as one of the chief malefactors and emphasized his radicalism by quoting the more sensational passages from the "socialistic" speech of 1891 and his 1893 Fourth of July oration.[23]

Doster seldom attempted to answer those who criticized his actions and political philosophy. He did not hesitate, however, to defend the course taken by his party. When Hoch's *Record* blamed the Populist legislators for the defeat of the Republican-sponsored Greenlee railroad regulation bill, Doster offered a vigorous denial. Hoch, he charged, had suppressed the truth when he wrote that the Populists voted against the reform measure because they wanted to keep an appointive railroad commission rather than accept an elective body as provided by the Greenlee bill. Doster argued that the bill was

Frank Doster as a member of the
1872 Kansas state legislature.

Dickinson County Populists on the way to a meeting in the
early 1890's. "Willowdale for John Davis."

Editor E. W. Hoch during the "legislative war" of 1893, drawn by Myron Waterman, best-known Kansas Populist cartoonist.
"Hoch of Marion. Mr. Speakah!
We are threaghtened with a dire calamity."
(Courtesy University of Kansas Libraries)

Frank Doster in 1896, when elected Chief Justice of the Kansas Supreme Court.

Political cartoon from the Topeka *Mail and Breeze* for June 28, 1901.

Chase County Courthouse, Cottonwood
Falls, Kansas; one of those in
which Doster presided.

Judge Frank Doster at the time of the First World War.

instead an attempt to retain the present Republican commissioners in office by legislative enactment, because it provided for elective commissioners *after* the terms of the incumbents had expired. The commissioners ("a coterie of servile corporation tools") had, moreover, refused to quit their offices and duties after Lewelling had removed them. Such an action, said Doster, degraded the executive prerogative. Doster also pointed out that a Populist-backed railroad bill had incorporated the elective principle. A final reason for the Populist opposition to the bill was that it set the date for the election of the commissioners on an off year when the rural vote would be light.[24]

In the summer of 1893 the Lewelling administration once again employed the legal talents of the Marion attorney. This time Doster was called upon to play a leading role in the epilogue of the "legislative war" farce. The disobedient militia officer J. W. F. Hughes had to be punished and humiliated. On July 19 the Governor wrote a terse note to Doster: "I want to see you come up at once if practicable. Of course you will be here tomorrow." Doster complied and upon his arrival in Topeka Lewelling commissioned him Judge Advocate General of the Kansas National Guard with the rank of major. In this capacity he was to conduct the court-martial of the recalcitrant Colonel Hughes.[25]

Hughes was ordered to appear before a five-man court. The Judge Advocate General created a sensation by appearing in court dressed in an infantry blouse, cavalry trousers, and a straw hat. Hughes stood accused on four charges: disobeying the orders of a superior officer; inducing others in the military service of the state to "misbehave before the enemy"; giving intelligence to the enemy; and conducting himself "to the prejudice of good order and military discipline, and demeanor unbecoming a gentleman and soldier." The Colonel pleaded not guilty to all charges and specifications, but the officers of the court (a majority of whom were Populists) found the defendant guilty on the first and fourth charges and sentenced him "to be dishonorably discharged from the military service of the state of Kansas." The angry Hughes later accused Doster of acting as prosecutor rather than as a judge advocate and of refusing to allow testimony to be brought into court. He also alleged that Lewelling was dictating to the court. The ludicrous proceedings lasted for thirty days and cost the state a total of $1,821.33.[26]

Doster served the Populist administration in other ways. In June, he, Jerry Simpson, and twenty-four other delegates were appointed to represent the state at the Lincoln, Nebraska, Railroad Congress.[27] But Doster's most effective service to his party continued to be as an orator. On the Fourth of July he delivered a major address to a Populist rally in his home community. The Marion *Times* commented that it was "needless to say that the large audience was held together until the last words fell from Judge Doster's lips oblivious to the artellery [*sic*] of the boys elsewhere in the park."[28]

The oration was centered around a definition of equality and the relationship of government to it. He began by saying that the Declaration of Independence was the first great document to proclaim the equal rights of mankind. The Magna Carta was but a reiteration of the privileges of the nobles and clergy. The Petition of Right was "little more than an admission of the right of the people to petition the king and other ruling branches of the government for a redress of grievances," and the Declaration of Rights was similarly incomplete with regard to equality.

Although the Declaration of Independence asserted the equality of all men there was still an inadequate understanding of equality and how it was to be attained. Certainly, he argued, it did not mean the "equality which belongs to the state of nature, because all law[,] all organization[,] all government is for the purpose of escaping from the inequalities and tyrannies of the natural state." Doster rejected the assertion that equality was one's fair share of the earth's goods, based on an event start in life, because "If so it is the equality of wild beasts, and the doctrine of the survival of the fittest is proved and exemplified in social as well as political life, and becomes established among the theories of constitutional government." Governments did not exist to perpetuate the inequalities inherent in the natural state. Quite the contrary: "All government and all necessity for government grows out of the fact of inequalities and that government which does not provide for the leveling and equalizing of the conditions which grow out of the unrestricted exercise of the natural powers of its citizens has failed in the purpose of its creation." More emphatically, he declared that the "necessary condition we call equality must be realized through the process of human government, and it is the business of government to discover and enforce those laws of harmony which raise man above the barbarous antagonisms of the natural state into relationships of social unity and fraternity." All laws of civilized nations were designed to repress, not encourage, individual action. Liberty was not the removal of restrictions, but the exact opposite. To illustrate, Doster held up the regulation of the liquor traffic as an example. As further proof of his belief in the duty of government to regulate for the common good, he cited Chief Justice Waite's opinion in the *Munn* case which held that property "clothed in the public interest" was subject to public control.

Doster finished his remarks on a humanitarian and optimistic note:

> I know that the world has set its face toward the humanities
> of life. I know that the equality of man means something more
> than equal privileges in money getting. I know that personal
> liberty does not mean selling hell in "original packages" to
> the heedless and weak. I know that the millionaire must go
> like the feudal lord has done. I know that the wail of the
> orphan is heard louder in the courts of heaven than the
> chuckling glee of the money changers. I know that humanity
> is above property, and that profit making on the bread of
> poverty is an abomination in the sight of the Lord.

In the course of the speech Doster had digressed to make a
scathing attack on the plutocratic enemy:

> Do you know, Sir Stupid, that while you have been following
> your sodden daily round of eating and drinking and sleeping,
> and buying and selling, and practicing the chicane and arti-
> fice of trade, a million of men have arisen who boldly chal-
> lenge the conscience of your life and the utility of your
> methods; who denounce your political economy as a sham
> and a fraud; who say that your laws of supply and demand
> no longer have application in the marts of trade; who laugh
> at your idea of over production and call it under consump-
> tion; who deny the beneficence of your law of division of
> labor, and say that machinery and not men now performs
> the labor; and who ridicule your theorizing about mutuality
> between labor and capital; who offset your statistics of in-
> crease of wealth by statistics of increase of those who lack
> bread and a place whereon to lay their heads; who declare
> that money is useless; that a condition of indebtedness is a
> condition of slavery; that a wage earner does not sell his
> labor but sells himself; that rent is robbery; that there can in
> the law of nature be no private property in land; that com-
> munism tends to the elimination of avarice and crime.

It was this paragraph which the Republican press was to use
so often to denounce the "communistic assistant Governor."
The phrase "rent is robbery" in particular gave the opposition
further evidence of his radicalism. It can be seen that he was

not making an explicit declaration of his own beliefs; he merely said that a "million of men" had laid down this and other challenges to the capitalistic system. As usual, however, Doster did not bother to offer an immediate defense or explanation of his meaning.

That fall, despite Doster's efforts, Republicans again swept the election for county officials. Populism suffered similar defeats throughout Kansas. The legislative war had done much to demoralize the party. Then too, the Republicans were busily quieting the dissension within their own ranks which had been brought on largely by the success of the "young crowd" in nominating A. W. ("Farmer") Smith for governor in 1892. The "old crowd," led by Cyrus Leland, was reasserting its power. At the same time, it was evident that the People's party was badly split. After attaining power in 1893, the differences between the leading men and women of the party came to the surface. Quarrels developed over patronage, policy, and ideology.[29]

The old cohesion they had known as members of a crusading opposition party was gone. In an atmosphere of hostility and pessimism, the Populists held their state convention in the summer of 1894. As a delegate, Frank Doster played a prominent part in getting a woman-suffrage plank incorporated in the platform. Others warned that an endorsement of the franchise for women would cause a loss of the votes of the foreign-born. Germans and Irish were especially opposed to it since they feared that prohibition would be strengthened as a result. Doster replied that principle was more important than playing for the votes of the various ethnic groups.[30]

Another major issue was a resolution condemning the anti-Catholic, anti-foreign American Protective Association. Whether Doster supported the resolution has not been ascertained, but it passed. A Populist lawyer complained to Lewelling that the woman-suffrage plank and the condemnation of the APA meant the alienation of both the foreigners and the nativists. "I was in hopes we would be left free to go before the people on the vital issues of the day but Doster and [Ben S.] Henderson were in the saddle and rode our party to the Devil in that Convention."[31]

Doster caused more eyebrow-raising in an address to the delegates which seemed most uncharacteristic of him. He asked them "to make a platform that talks less about free silver and more about salvation; less about finance and more about religion." He did not want a platform designed to catch votes; instead he wanted one "that had God almighty in it." "You may put in it if you will that we are in favor of silver at a ratio of 16 to 1, but I want principles in it by which we can live more acceptably in the sight of the Lord." Strange talk indeed from Marion's village atheist![32]

After the convention Doster took to the stump. He made his major pronouncement in the campaign in Topeka on Labor Day. Prefacing his remarks with a reminder that the hard times and discontent were universal, he denied that they resulted from "some malignant and uncontrollable force operating in the physical or moral worlds." Political parties and political administration could mitigate the distress, and "Unless it be conceded that such is true there is no excuse for the existence of political parties." The old parties, however, had failed to adapt to the "strange conditions" which the industrial age had thrust upon society. Protection and the "honest dollar" were totally insufficient to cure the depressed condition of the people.

The Populist party alone, said Doster, had committed itself to the full use of government in order to construct a just social and economic system for the new age. "The Populist party proposes as the only means to the desired end to utilize the power of the combined whole, to bring the power of the social mass to bear upon rebellious individuals who . . . menace the peace and safety of the state." Monopolies and trusts whose operations were "clothed in the public interest" were "in reality the functions and agencies of government itself." They must, therefore, be controlled or owned by the people. Railroads, like highways, schools, and armies, "should be treated as public in character." Since recent decisions had shown that the courts were not to be relied upon to uphold railroad regulation laws, public ownership was the only solution.

As the "philosophical bases" for positive governmental action, Doster offered "two political formulae": "One that it is the business of government to do that for the individual which he cannot successfully do for himself and which other individuals will not do for him upon just or equitable terms; and the other that the industrial system of a nation, like its political system, should be a government of and for and by the people alone."[33]

Doster's public statements after 1894 tended to be both less radical and less abstract. The Labor Day speech of that year was the last major address for some time to come in which he appeared to espouse bold ideas; perhaps a desire for high political office caused him to make more temperate and commonplace utterances.

The 1894 election brought defeat for the Populists, but during the administration of Republican Governor E. N. Morrill, the young crowd–old crowd feud broke out anew. Now it was the Republican party which suffered most from internal dissension. The Populists had a good chance of regaining control of the state in 1896, particularly because there was a strong possibility of fusion with the Democrats (who had put up their own state ticket in 1894).

In the spring of 1896, a reporter for the Abilene *Chronicle* sounded out Frank Doster on the likelihood of fusion. "Yes," he replied, "in the same sense as there was in '92. The Populists will nominate the electors and they will be indorsed by the Democrats. There will be no division of state offices." With fusion, he added, McKinley could not expect to carry Kansas. Perhaps with an eye toward pleasing the Democrats, Doster gave the *Chronicle* man his views on the tariff: "The idea that a protective tariff will relieve the financial stringency is fallacious. I only hope the free silver men in congress will be wise enough to permit tariff legislation to again demonstrate the inutility of the _____ thing. Of all the colossal humbugs, the protective cry is the worst."[34]

As the date for the state convention drew near, the Topeka *Capital* reported that the Marion attorney had been in Topeka "looking after his campaign for United States Senator." The *Capital* assured its readers that Doster had given up a previous ambition for the nomination for chief justice; despite Doster's denial that he was seeking any office, he would "calmly wait for developments with the hope that something will happen to turn the tide for Senator in his direction."[35]

Leaving his precise plans a mystery, Doster left in July for St. Louis where he was to sit as a delegate to the national People's party convention. Like most other leading Kansas Populists he was in favor of endorsing Bryan's candidacy. Still he was unwilling to let the Democracy swallow his party completely. His colleague W. A. Harris seconded the nomination of Sewall, the Democratic choice for vice-president; Doster, however, was among those who wanted Tom Watson as Bryan's running mate so that the People's party could retain a separate identity. After the Georgian's name had been placed in nomination, Doster gave a seconding speech. When he expressed his belief that Sewall would withdraw if Watson received the Populist nomination, cries of "Good" were heard in the convention hall. The southern delegates in particular applauded his sentiments. The majority of the Kansas delegates stayed with Sewall, but the convention chose Watson as the Populist nominee for vice-president.[36]

Upon returning to Kansas, Doster still refrained from announcing his candidacy for any office. As the Kansas Populists were gathering in Abilene for their state convention, it was generally believed that he aspired to the Senate seat. Soon, however, reports from Marion County reached them which indicated that a member of the county's delegation would place his name before the convention as a candidate for chief justice. In letting his wishes be known at such a late date, Doster had endangered his chances. One of the other contenders, George W. Clark, was said to have a majority of pledged delegates.[37]

On the opening day of the convention, the Populists first endorsed the Bryan-Watson ticket. The agenda next called for a report from the conference committee, but since the committee was not ready to report, the convention voted to suspend the rules and begin nominating candidates for state offices. First on the schedule was the chief justiceship. Henry McLean of Marion County nominated Doster ("whose very name is an epitome of all that is near and dear to the people of Kansas"). Former Attorney General Little gave a seconding speech. Three other men were also nominated: Clark, W. C. Webb, ad M. B. Nicolson. The delegates then passed a resolution requiring all four contenders to appear before the convention to speak.

When Doster's turn came he dropped a rhetorical bombshell

not soon forgotten by the Republican opposition. He promised his fellow Populists that: "If elected, though hampered by technical decisions in the interests of wealth, I will diligently search the books to find some law through which the interests of the common people may be subserved." However offensive the remark was to the ears of conservatives, it was reported that as he left the platform "the delegates rose as one man and cheered." Following the addresses of the other candidates, the balloting began. Before half the roll had been called, delegations began changing their votes to Doster. "The effect was electric," said the Topeka *Capital*. When the Smith county delegation cast its votes, he had the nomination. At this point, state Senator H. G. Jumper offered a motion that the nomination be made unanimous, "which carried amid tremendous enthusiasm." A dozen delegates then escorted "the idol of the convention" to the platform where he "modestly" expressed his thanks.

The nomination of Frank Doster was held up by the opposition as the supreme example of Populist perversity. According to the Republicans, no greater evil could befall the state than the elevation of this "communist" to the highest court of the state. His promise to "find some law" to benefit the masses was taken as a threat to invent laws.[38]

Among the most vituperative foes of Populism and all its works was editor-novelist E. W. Howe of the Atchison *Globe*. He took particular delight in attacking the party's nominee for chief justice. "Doster," wrote the "Sage of Potato Hill," "is an anarchist and socialist of the first class, and about as fit to be chief justice of Kansas as a hog is to teach polite manners." As for Doster's theory on the paramount rights of the user, it had "hanged more horse thieves than ever died in any other way." Howe charged that one of the Populist dignitaries,

Judge William F. Rightmire, considered Doster's candidacy an "awful dose." "If Doster is an 'awful dose' for a man like Rightmire," said Howe, "he is a worse one for better men." According to Howe, Rightmire had also insinuated "terrible things about Doster's reputation for honesty." In denouncing Tom Watson, the Atchison editor took a swipe at Doster and other Populists: "Watson is your true Populist. He is as clownish as Simpson, as hare-brained as our senior senator [Peffer], as vicious as Doster and as uncouth as Leedy."[39]

As always, E. W. Hoch of Marion was ready to speak out against the local "socialist." After the St. Louis convention, Hoch's *Record* chided Doster for playing a part in the Populist surrender to Bryan. When Doster was nominated at Abilene, Hoch solemnly wrote: "This will make socialism the chief issue in Kansas this year." In a long letter to the Topeka *Capital* the Marion editor wrote that although tempted to be proud of the candidacy of a fellow townsman, he could never forget the "socialistic" remarks of 1891. He agreed that Doster's latest pronouncements were primarily about the monetary problem, but charged that he had never been enthusiastic about silver and that at heart he was still a socialist. Hoch once again defended his earlier support of Doster for district judge: that was before Doster had gone "daft on socialism, populism and other fool isms."[40]

The best known attack on Doster and his colleagues during the campaign of 1896 was by a chubby, young, and relatively unknown Emporia editor. "What's the Matter with Kansas" was published in the August 15 issue of his *Gazette*. The editorial was a masterpiece of invective, and its adoption as a campaign tract by Mark Hanna made William Allen White a national celebrity. In it he singled out the leading lights of Kansas Populism and castigated them individually, but without mentioning them by name. Leedy, the party's candidate for governor, was "an old mossback Jacksonian who snorts and howls because there is a bathtub in the State house"; J. D. Botkin, nominee for congressman-at-large, was "an old human hoop skirt" who had been raked up from the "ash heap of failure"; Louis Boyle, candidate for attorney general, was "a kid without a law practice"; Annie L. Diggs and Mary E. Lease were "harpies" sent out to tell the nation that "Kansas is raising hell and letting the corn go to weed." His characterization of Doster was equally biting: "We have another shabby, wild-eyed, rattle-brained fanatic who has said openly in a dozen speeches that 'the rights of the user are paramount to the rights of the owner'; we are running him for chief justice, so that capital will come tumbling over itself to get into the state."

White was no reactionary. Like Hoch and several other rising young Republicans he preferred to bring about reform through established party channels. To them, the Populists, like the "old crowd" Republicans, were relics of the Civil War generation, out of tune with modern society and its needs. In time, however, White was to acknowledge Progressivism's debt to Populism and single out Doster as one of the major prophets of the new age of reform.

The Democratic and Silver Republican conventions of the summer of 1896 endorsed the People's party ticket, including Doster. Still his candidacy was a "bitter pill" for many old-line Democrats. Howe's *Globe* stated that the Marion radical was "exactly the man the Democrats do not want." Some of them refused to swallow Populism and justified their decision on the grounds that those heading the Populist ticket were totally unacceptable. In Topeka three hundred Democrats formed a club to support Republican Governor Morrill's bid for reelection. A member of the organization declared that: "The self-respecting Democrats are not going to vote for J. W. Leedy for Governor or for Frank Doster for Chief Justice. The man who loves his State and respects its institutions can never cast a ballot for a turbulent demagogue on the one hand, or an avowed socialist on the other."[41] Another disgruntled group was the nonfusing "middle-of-the-road" Populists. It ran a separate slate of presidential electors, but not, however, for state officers.

The Republican ticket was composed largely of Morrill administration incumbents, except for T. F. Garver, who replaced Chief Justice David Martin as the nominee to face Doster. It was said that Martin was "soft" on free silver. He had, moreover, made himself unpopular with his party by ruling that chairman Briedenthal could retain his office as State Bank Commissioner after the overthrow of the Populists in 1894.[42]

Doster opened his campaign in late August at a bipartisan gathering in Atchison, where he shared the platform with former Senator Ingalls. As he was to do for most of the campaign, the Populist nominee confined his remarks to the monetary question. A few days later, at Kansas City's Huron Place, he made an old soldier's condemnation of the Republican party. "I used to be a Republican. I respected the party of Lincoln. If Republicanism was what it was once, when it grabbed the flag thrown down by treason and hugged it to its bared breast, I would be a Republican yet. I love the party of those days, but I have nothing but contempt for it now."

The Huron Place speech was also the occasion of an explanation of his notorious "rights-of-the-user" statement of 1891. "What I referred to was where a person or corporation had dedicated property to the use of the people. In that I said just what Justice Waite of the supreme court decided many years ago [in *Munn* v. *Illinois*]. Telegraph, telephone, railroad, and like companies dedicate their property to the public, and in such cases I am willing to stand by my assertion. . . . I still maintain my position as before, and at the same time I declare that I am not an anarchist."[43]

In a two-hour address before a Topeka audience of nine hundred, he returned to the free-silver theme. Opponents of bimetallism had advanced the argument that silver currency degraded labor, citing Mexico as an example. Doster replied that Mexican currency was worth less because of the inferior skill and intelligence of the Mexican laborer. "American labor commands the American dollar, Mexican labor commands the Mexican dollar."[44]

In another Topeka speech Doster repudiated the notion that the "crime of '73" had caused depressed conditions. He contended that domestic legislation alone could not have brought about a world-wide economic catastrophe. Rather it was a "series of crimes of the same character committed about the same time by the countries of Europe as well." When Doster repeated these sentiments before a Populist rally in his home town, editor Hoch pointed out the inconsistency of proposing a national remedy, free silver, for what he had admitted were international ills. [45]

Doster's dilemma in the 1896 campaign was that for the good of his party and his own candidacy, he felt obliged to speak on concrete issues of the day rather than dwell on the abstractions with which he was more comfortable. At the same time, the Republicans constantly reminded the voters of his earlier "radical" utterances. The Lawrence *Journal* observed that "Mr. Doster has not repudiated his declaration to the effect that the 'rights of the user are paramount to the rights of the owner.' If he adheres to his theory he ought to secure the votes of every horse thief, every chicken thief, every embezzler, every cattle thief, every swindler in the whole state."The Topeka *Capital* quoted a passage from his 1892 *Agora* article and branded it "rank socialism."[46]

For the remainder of the campaign Doster doggedly stayed with the currency question. After listening to a two-hour Doster speech on silver at Leavenworth, a journalist found him "conservative in a degree that was disappointing to some who went to hear a radical talk." In the closing days of October he delivered similar speeches at a Lawrence free-silver barbecue and a Hutchinson rally.[47]

During the electioneering the Republicans raised yet another issue detrimental to Doster. While on duty in the Stevens County "war" he had been a district judge as well as a militia captain. After his period of active service he had filed a voucher for compensation for twelve days' service at five dollars a day. The Republican administration disallowed his claim on the grounds that no state judge could receive fees or other remuneration from the state except for his judicial salary. In 1893, the Republicans charged, Doster reapplied for payment to the Populist state treasurer, claiming that the original voucher had been lost, and received the sixty dollars. Not only was he a "socialist" and insincere about silver, he was now accused of personal dishonesty.[48]

The Republicans also sought to embarass the Democratic allies of the Populists by pointing out that they had once denounced Doster and his cohorts in the strongest terms. The *Capital* reprinted David Overmeyer's anti-Doster address of 1891. Now, said the *Capital,* Overmeyer was supporting Doster for an even higher post.[49]

In addition to the Republican attacks, bickering among the

Populists themselves endangered their chances for victory. Late in the campaign a quarrel developed between Doster and chairman Briedenthal. In a letter to W. D. Vincent, Briedenthal expressed his exasperation with the judicial candidate. Doster, he wrote, had at first declined to fill speaking engagements in the western part of the state because he believed it unnecessary. He wanted instead to attend a Grand Army of the Republic reunion in Topeka. Briedenthal had been able to dissuade him, telling Doster that he would be hooted down and humiliated by the veterans, and when Doster finally began stumping western Kansas he complained that the Populists had been neglecting it. Briedenthal also told Vincent of his refusal to follow Doster's suggestion that the party apply to the Democratic state committee for funds. Another episode which irritated the chairman was Doster's attempt to vindicate his actions in the sixty-dollar-claim affair. Briedenthal believed that "the less said about it the better" and refused to publish Doster's defense of himself. Had Briedenthal's letter remained private it would have been of little consequence; but it fell into Republican hands and the *Capital* gleefully published it in the October 24 issue.

The Populists experienced further difficulties when Tom Watson's appearance in the state threatened to disrupt fusion. In a series of three Kansas speeches the Georgian inveighed against Sewall and the Democratic party. The opposition press gave much publicity to his harangues. Doster, however, believed that fusion was being strengthened by the Republican attempts to split the alliance of the Populists and Democrats: "It is a good thing to have the hoops driven down, for it drives us closer together."[50]

Throughout the campaign Doster was the chief target of the Republican attacks on Populist candidates. Only Bryan received more attention in the columns of the city dailies. At the close of the campaign the *Capital* issued a grave warning: "Under existing conditions, no greater disaster could come to Kansas than the election of Frank Doster." The efforts of the Republicans were to no avail. Bryan carried the state handily and the fusion ticket was swept into office. Doster, running behind only Leedy and Botkin, easily defeated Garver, 167,920 to 159,428.[51]

After the election the city newspapers were less prone to the hysterical denunciation of the triumphant Populists. The Topeka *State Journal* published a calm interview with the victorious Frank Doster, then staying at the National Hotel in the capital city. The *Journal* reporter observed that "The hard work of the campaign has left no trace upon his features. They are as immovable as ever. He does not seem to be affected by the result of the election. His demeanor would have been the same if he had been defeated." At the hotel his friends were having "considerable sport" introducing him as "the only anarchist ever elected to the supreme bench." The reporter noted that Doster never smiled at these pleasantries and although he shook hands warmly with those pouring in to congratulate him, he did not join the conversations going on around him. Indeed, said the *Journal,* "No one ever heard Judge Doster 'joke' and not many have seen him smile." When asked if he was surprised at the outcome of the election in Kansas, he replied that he had thought the victory would be even more decisive.

The interviewer then moved to a more important question: Did the Judge wish to comment about the charges that he was a dangerous man to have on the Supreme Court? "No, I have little to say," answered Doster in a low voice. "They were simply campaign stories and were not believed by the people who told them. They preferred Judge Garver to me and they took that means to express their preference." Were his views on the law at variance with those of the majority of the legal profession? "No sir, I know only one code of law and that is the same one studied by the other lawyers and I shall try to follow it as best I can."[52]

The Topeka *Capital* conducted a similar interview. Doster told the reporter "Physically I am tired; politically I am satisfied." He was, however, "very sorry" about the defeat of Bryan. "I think he is the greatest leader of men this country has ever known. . . . He is the Rienze [*sic*] of the American people, but unlike that Roman character he will not fall." Again he was asked if his views had been misrepresented. Doster replied that while his attitudes on legal subjects had not been distorted, his opinions on political and social questions certainly had been. He denied that he ever said "rent is robbery" and again explained that his "rights of the user" doctrine applied only to quasi-public utilities such as railroads. Once more he assured the public that he knew "no law different from what the profession generally has learned." He added, however, that "many of the recent decisions have been along lines of new legal departure, extorted from the courts by the capitalistic institutions of the country. If I have any views at all different from that of everybody else it is that we need a return to the old ways and the old common law precedents. They will be found more consonant with theories of popular right at least."[53]

Here Doster was suggesting an unusual reform approach: strict adherence to the ancient principles of the common law. Perhaps this is the answer to the paradox posed by his rhetorical radicalism and legal conservatism. Tom Watson told the Georgia farmers that the common law was an instrument of reaction and oppression.[54] Doster, on the other hand, found social justice inherent in the Anglo-American legal tradition. His pledge to "find some law" to benefit the common people did not mean then that he would manufacture his own law. Rather it was a promise to rediscover principles and precedents beneficial to the people.

In the weeks between the election and the inauguration of the Populist officials, the opposition press took pains to point out that many of them were not so bad after all. The Topeka *State Journal* assured its readers that "Mr Doster is powerless to put his doctrines into practice and he holds his views merely theoretically." Ed Howe's *Globe* allowed that the Chief Justice-elect was in a good position to do well because most bad judicial decisions were the results of judges showing favoritism to their lawyer friends. There were few Populist lawyers and therefore Doster had few friends to favor. He had been "so much abused that little [was] expected of him." Former Senator Ingalls was quick to point out that he was not alarmed at the Populist victory. They were, after all, Anglo-Saxons and had the same genius for self-government as others of the race. As for the new Chief Justice, Ingalls described him as a former Republican and "a man of high private character and professional attainments."[55]

In a letter to Governor-elect Leedy's home town newspaper, Doster tried to allay the fears of the more conservative citizens by offering a full explanation of his "rights of the user" remark. As quoted by opponents it was "a garbled extract taken from a public address of several years ago, wrested from its context, perverted in meaning and deprived of the benefit of all accompanying explanatory language. Its circulation in the partisan press is an apt instance of the truth of the old proverb that 'half a truth is a whole lie.' " He had, it was true, said that the rights of the user were paramount to those of the owner, but

he had employed the words "use" and "ownership" inter-
changeably with "labor" and "capital" and had made a distinction between kinds of capital.[56]

Immediately after the election the Kansas City *Star*
lamented the victory of Doster, who was "an Altgeld on a
diminished scale."[57] A few weeks later, the *Star* sent a reporter
to Marion for what a later generation of journalists would call
an "in-depth" interview. The result, surprisingly, was a reveal-
ing and sympathetic picture of the unconventional village
lawyer once so roundly vilified by the *Star*.

Traveling through Marion County, the reporter found the
area had "big, prosperous looking dwellings on one part, with
imperial farms and 47,000 acres of the Scully lands in the
other." In Marion he sought the Doster home which was located on a hill having "many pretty and even pretentious
houses," but, to his surprise, he discovered that the Chief Justice-elect and his family lived in a frame cottage much in need
of paint and repairs. "It stands alongside a big, comfortable
home. The iron fence and neat lawn of the big house adjoin
the uncared-for grounds and shaky picket fence of the Doster
cottage. The contrast is sharp." He later learned that the milk
can hanging on the gate was there because Doster's wife and
children ran an "amateur dairy" with a small herd of Jersey
cows. At the house he found only Caroline Doster. He noted
that she had a reputation for brilliance in Marion and had
been "active in literary and agnostic societies." "For several
years," however, "the Judge and his wife have been secluded in
their home."

Informed by Mrs. Doster that her husband was downtown,
the journalist walked to the business district. Passing a barber
shop he "caught a glimpse of a thin, smoothly shaven, sallow
face within. It was a face out of place amid plain and rural

surroundings. It would do for a martyr with the flames licking the high brow." The writer then noticed the strange man take the brush from the barber's hand and brush his "scant hair" himself—"as Mr. Bryan always does." The *Star* man guessed that he was looking at Judge Frank Doster, "the ablest and chosen exponent of Populism in Kansas." As he approached Doster he saw his face "light up in a smile like a brief flash of sunshine through the clouds," but "then he relapsed into gloom." He noticed "a number of paradoxical characteristics" in the man. "He looks both old and young. He has a delicate, nervous physiognomy. He avoids society. His townsmen say he never speaks unless sopken to. He wears a perpetual mask of melancholy. Upon close view he is a well preserved man, approaching fifty; at a careless glance he looks like a young man at thirty after a hard life."

The reporter's description of Doster's habits of dress confirms at least one point of William Allen White's vitriolic characterization of a few months earlier; the Chief Justice-elect was decidely shabby. "He wears his soft hat cocked askew on his Indian black hair, and a 'stand-up' collar gaping widely in front and wrapped by a 'string' tie that is tied in a little close knot—not a bow—with the ends hanging down eight inches over his shirt bosom. The three upper buttons of his waistcoat are always unbuttoned. He wears boxed-toed shoes, a cheap suit and a big gold watch chain. He has always dressed just this way."

The journalist saw before him an example of how quickly failure could turn to success in America. Before the election Doster was a forty-eight-year-old lawyer who had experienced a string of political reverses. "His youth, with its high hopes, was gone forever. However, instead of encountering final defeat, this dark and sad-faced man at Marion was carried to the pinnacle of success."

He was a strange figure whom even his neighbors did not understand. "He has been called a Socialist by men who know him and an anarchist by men who don't know him. This is because he has no classification. Not being an anarchist, or a socialist, or a calamity howler, or a demagogue[,] all known classifications fail." He was a "mysterious character" to the reporter, but at the same time he looked upon his subject as possibly the prophet of a new social order. "Ex-Governor Altgeld, Senator Tillman, Mrs. Lease, Goveror Stone, Governor Pennoyer, Governor Pingree and Tom Watson have failed to create a new classification. They are agitators and disturbers, not reformers; haranguers, not students; messengers of evil, not physicians with succor. Doster is not one of them nor part of them." Although Doster had at various times advocated Greenbackism, Populism, and free silver, he did so, the writer believed, for political expediency. His actual philosophy transcended these narrow, often cranky movements.

Since Doster was about to depart for Topeka, the reporter decided to accompany him on the train in quest of more of the Judge's views. Naturally enough, he wanted Doster's explanation of the famous speech of 1891. He first told Doster that "around the hotel stoves" of Marion the people interpreted his remarks about the rights of the user to mean that a landlord and tenant "should be partners and share the vicissitudes of using the land"; that if a crop failed the tenant should not be compelled to pay the rent. Doster replied that he had never made such a proposition and it was "certainly out of the pale of the law." "Nor," he added, "am I prepared to say it is a moral right." The journalist then shifted his questions to the cause of widespread discontent in Kansas. To draw out his opinions, the reporter suggested to Doster that the hard times were brought on by the ease of borrowing in times of prosperity and the inability to pay debts in periods of depression. Doster responded in a slow and deliberate manner: "It would have been far better for the people of Kansas had they never been able to borrow money." "The elevation of money-lending to the chief business of mankind," he continued, "is responsible for the disorders and discontent. It is an entirely modern development. It is a great evil that produces waves of expansion followed by wreck and ruin. It must be checked."

When asked how he would change conditions, Doster replied that he had "certain ideas, certain plans, which I believe will avail, but I am not willing to make them public now through the press." At that point Doster referred the reporter to a friend of his on the train who had a plan for repudiating municipal bonds. He then pulled the gentleman into a seat near the reporter and fled to another part of the train. Not until they reached Topeka was the journalist able to continue the interview. There Doster offered his now familiar defense of the so-called socialistic speech of 1891, saying that he was speaking specifically about corporations doing business of a public nature. His doctrines meant neither confiscation nor repudiation.[58]

The unknown reporter for the *Star* had not solved any of the mysteries surrounding the Marion lawyer, but he did succeed in presenting an objective sketch of a complex, misunderstood man. The Topeka *Capital,* which, like the *Star,* had been hostile to Doster in the campaign, also printed an article on him. Here again the writer was puzzled but fair-minded. "Nobody knows a great deal about Doster. The inner man is locked securely from the world." One of his lawyer colleagues ("an intimate friend as Doster's intimacies go") was quoted as saying: "Doster and I have been warm friends for years, but I know very little about him. The man lives within a shell." No one, wrote the *Capital* reporter, knew what, if any, aspirations Doster harbored in his soul; nor was anyone outside his family asked to share either his sorrows or joys. "He is as imperturbable as a hitching post, and so far as visible signs go, as callous to emotion as a leaf torn from the Statutes of 1897." But those closest to Doster were convinced that "beneath his calm, passionless exterior there runs a broad, deep vein of human sympathy, tinctured with kindliness and healthful sentiment, and banked by an attitude of even and exact justice to all men."[59]

Whatever lingering doubts the opposition may have had, an immense crowd of Populists and Democrats gathered at Representative Hall in Topeka to witness the inauguration. By the start of the ceremony, the hall was packed by what was estimated to be the largest number of people ever to attend a Kansas inaugural. They had good reason to be enthusiastic. The fusionists had elected all their candidates for state office and had clear majorities in both houses of the legislature. With the election of Doster they had a Populist majority on the Supreme Court as well.

Retiring Chief Justice Martin administered the oath to the incoming officials. He offered all of them an opportunity to kiss the Bible. Only three out of eight (Leedy, Auditor William H. Morris, and Treasurer David H. Heflebower) accepted. Doster was the last to be sworn in. At this point Martin offered his congratulations: "The last duty of my official term as chief justice is a most pleasant one, for I feel that the office is well bestowed and that you are in every respect worthy and well chosen for the office to which you have been called by the suffrage of the people." It may have been sweet revenge for the outgoing Chief Justice to praise his Populist successor, for Martin had been dumped by his fellow Republicans in their 1896 convention. But perhaps as a jurist he was well aware of Doster's ability and was simply giving his honest appraisal and sincere good wishes.

After Doster took his oath he accepted a large cluster of flowers sent by a friend and prepared to leave the platform. As he was doing so "the entire crowd raised a cry for a speech and Mr. Doster was compelled to return and speak a few words." He told his admirers that he was unprepared and would only endorse the "patriotic" and "loyal" remarks of Leedy and outgoing Governor Morrill. Unaware that the new Chief Justice was addressing the crowd, the artillerymen outside fired the first salvo of their salute to the new administration. At the close of the inaugural Leedy and Doster repaired to the Governor's office where they received well-wishers for two hours.[60]

The new regime was in an excellent position to bring about the reforms they had championed for the last seven years. Populists also expected much of their new Chief Justice and many of them believed that he was on the bench for the purpose of revolutionizing the Kansas system of jurisprudence —so did some fearful Republicans. At the party's annual Kansas Day Club meeting, young Henry J. Allen (later a Bull-Mooser and reform governor) told his fellow Republicans that "until he has done something to prove to the contrary, I believe that Frank Doster, though he be Chief Justice of Kansas, is no safer guide to the destinies of a state than was the Populist lecturer who taught the doctrine of the rights of the user."[61] Neither the Populists nor the Republicans, however, could predict with certainty the course Doster would take. For the next six years the inscrutable man from Marion was to surprise both his supporters and his detractors.

NOTES

[1]Topeka *Capital,* Aug. 23, 1892.

[2]*The Agora,* II (Oct., 1892), 121.

[3]*Ibid.,* pp. 122–23.

[4]*Ibid.,* p. 126.

[5]*Ibid.*

[6]Quoted in the Marion *Record,* March 25 and Nov. 4, 1892.

[7]Powell Moore (ed.), "A Hoosier in Kansas: The Diary of Hiram H. Young, 1886–1895," *Kansas Historical Quarterly,* XIV (May, 1946), 442; J. K. Hudson, *Letters to Governor Lewelling* (Topeka: Topeka Capital Co., 1893), p. 73.

[8]Hudson, *Letters,* p. 140.

[9]*Scrap Book Containing the Proceedings of the Kansas State Legislature for the Session of 1893, As Published in the Topeka Daily Capital,* Prepared for C. S. Gleed, II, 54, 72, and 80, University of Kansas Library. (Hereafter cited as *Gleed Scrapbook.*)

[10]Marion *Record,* Jan. 13, 1893; *Gleed Scrapbook,* II, 62, 217, and 238.

[11]*Gleed Scrapbook,* I, 64, 128, 131, and 135.

[12]*Ibid.,* p. 149.

[13]*Ibid.,* pp. 154–55.

[14]*Ibid.,* pp. 160–62.

[15]Walter T. K. Nugent, *The Tolerant Populists: Kansas Populism and Nativism* (Chicago: University of Chicago Press, 1963), p. 146; *Kansas Farmer,* Feb. 1, 1893.

[16]*House Journal: Proceedings of the Legislative Assembly of the State of Kansas, Eighth Biennial Session* (Topeka: 1893), pp. 219–20, 231–32, and 239–40. (Hereafter cited as *House Journal.*)

[17]*Gleed Scrapbook,* I, 55.

[18]*Ibid.,* p. 238.

[19]Little to Lewelling, Feb. 17, 1893, Governors' Correspondence, Lorenzo D. Lewelling, "State Departments, Attorney General," Archives Division, Kansas State Historical Society.

[20]*Gleed Scrapbook,* I, 348 and 350.

[21]*House Journal,* pp. 764, 839, 873, and 910.

[22]*The Agora,* II (April, 1893), 275–99.

[23]Hudson, *Letters,* pp. 8, 14, and 32; E. W. Hoch, *The Last War: A Bloodless Battle for Constitutional Government; the Facts, the Law and the Equity* (Topeka: Republican State Headquarters, 1893), p. 9.

[24]Marion *Times,* July 13, 1893.

[25]Lewelling to Doster, July 19, 1893, Governors' Correspondence, 1893–94, Number 109, Archives Division, Kansas State Historical Society; Adjutant General of the State of Kansas, *Ninth Biennial Report* (Topeka: 1895), p. 36.

[26]Raymond C. Miller, "The Populist Party in Kansas" (Ph.D. dissertation, University of Chicago, 1928), p. 259; Adjutant General, *Sixteenth Biennial Report* (Topeka: 1909), pp. 257–58 and 261; and *Ninth Biennial Report,* p. 71.

[27]"Official State Roster," *Kansas Historical Collections,* VIII (1903–1904), 539.

[28]Marion *Times,* July 6, 1893.

[29]Marion *Record,* Nov. 10, 1893; Walter T. K. Nugent, "How the Populists Lost in 1894," *Kansas Historical Quarterly,* XXXI (Autumn, 1965), 245–55.

[30]Nugent, *The Tolerant Populists,* pp. 159–60.

[31]*Ibid.,* p. 167.

[32]Malin, *A Concern about Humanity: Notes on Reform, 1872–1912, at the National and Kansas Levels of Thought* (Lawrence, Kansas: The Author, 1964), p. 149.

[33]*Ibid.,* pp. 150–52; Topeka *Advocate,* Sept. 19, 1894; Norman Pollack, *The Populist Response to Industrial America; Midwestern Populist Thought* (New York: 1962), pp. 17–18.

[34]*Biographical Clippings,* D, II (Kansas State Historical Society), pp. 213–14.

[35]Topeka *Capital,* July 4, 1896.

[36]*Ibid.,* July 25, 1896.

[37]*Ibid.,* July 31, 1896.

[38]*Ibid.,* Aug. 7, 1896; Atchison *Globe,* Aug. 6, 1896; Miller, "The Populist Party in Kansas," p. 293.

[39]Atchison *Globe,* Aug. 7, Sept. 2, Oct. 20 and 26, 1896.

[40]Marion *Record,* July 31 and Aug. 7, 1896, and Nov. 19, 1897; Topeka *Capital,* Oct. 11, 1896.

[41]Atchison *Globe,* Aug. 6, 1896; Marion *Record,* Aug. 21, 1896.

[42]Topeka *Capital,* Aug. 11, 1896.

[43]*Ibid.,* Aug. 25 and 29, 1896.

[44]*Ibid.,* Aug. 30, 1896.

[45]Wellington *People's Voice,* Sept. 17, 1896; Marion *Record,* Sept. 11, 1896.

[46]Topeka *Capital,* Sept. 17 and Oct. 20, 1896.

[47]*Ibid.,* Oct. 18, 21, and 28, 1896.

[48]*Ibid.,* Oct. 10, 1896.

[49]*Ibid.,* Oct. 11, 1896.

[50]W. P. Harrington, "The Populist Party in Kansas," *Kansas Historical Collections,* XVI, 440.

[51]Topeka *Capital,* Oct. 29, 1896; Secretary of State of the State of Kansas, *Tenth Biennial Report* (Topeka: 1896), pp. 92–93.

[52]Topeka *State Journal,* Nov. 6, 1896.

[53]Topeka *Capital,* Nov. 7, 1896.

[54]C. Vann Woodward, *Tom Watson: Agrarian Rebel* (New York: Oxford University Press, 1963), pp. 172–73.

[55]Topeka *State Journal,* Nov. 26, 1896; Atchison *Globe,* Nov. 14 and 30, 1896.

[56]Topeka *State Journal,* Nov. 26, 1896.

[57]Kansas City *Star,* Nov. 6, 1896.

[58]*Ibid.,* Nov. 29, 1896.

[59]Topeka *Capital,* Nov. 26, 1896.

[60]*Ibid.,* Jan. 12, 1897; Emporia *Gazette,* Jan. 11, 1897.

[61]*The Kansas Day Club Addresses, 1892–1901* (Hutchinson, Kansas: W. Y. Morgan, 1901), p. 235.

4

IN THE SAME CAR—GOING UP

KANSAS reformers had every reason to be optimistic as the fusionist regime came into office in 1897. Control of the executive and legislative branches by the "Demo-Pops" augured well for the reform cause. They had, however, succeeded too well. As members of a ruling political coalition, they had to meet problems of patronage, policy, and ideological differences. Immediately, deep cleavages and personal antagonisms reappeared. Leedy's administration, like that of Lewelling, accomplished little.

The state Supreme Court was in a more favorable position to promote the announced goals of the Populists. Justices Allen and Doster constituted a majority on the three-man court. In addition, to aid and influence them, there were Annie L. Diggs as State Librarian (the library being an adjunct of the court) and G. C. Clemens as court reporter. But the radicals who hoped for revolutionary decisions from the supreme bench waited in vain. Both Doster and Allen were scholarly and orthodox lawyers. There was little difference between their opinions and those of the Republicans who served from 1897 to 1903. Then too, there was a Populist majority for only two years. In 1898 Allen was defeated for reelection by Republican William R. Smith. In 1900 a constitutional amendment increased the number of justices to seven and the four new members were all Republicans.

Chief Justice Doster, moreover, was more interested in improving the quality of the decisions coming from the Kansas courts than in using his position to promote radicalism. As early as 1893 he had lamented the fact that the decisions of the lower courts of Kansas were reversed more often than in any other state. He also pointed out that the decisions of the Kansas Supreme Court were seldom cited elsewhere. His chief objection was that the judges were guilty of unimaginative and slavish following of precedent. Since two cases were seldom alike, he called for "an effort to resolve cases by philosophical reasoning. . . . The faculties of comparison are less to be relied upon than those of original thought." For him this did not imply that a judge need be a liberal. Indeed, he cited former Kansas Justice David J. Brewer, then a leading conservative on the federal Supreme Court, as a "notable example" of broad thinking. "It is a pleasure to read some of his opinions. He was no legal parrot, but had a voice and vocabulary of his own."[1]

Doster's most marked characteristic as a jurist was his insistence on what is now called "judicial restraint." In an age in which courts tended to nullify regulatory legislation, his opinions in these matters make him appear friendly to liberal aims. In one of the earliest cases to appear before the Doster court, *In re Davis,* the question in point involved the right of the Populist legislature to establish a committee to investigate bribery of its members. His colleague Allen joined Republican William A. Johnston in denying the constitutionality of the act which, they believed, endowed the committee with judicial power. Doster wrote a vigorous dissent upholding the rights of the "popular branch" of government. He deplored the current tendency of the courts "to minimize the power of the legislative branch of government and magnify that of the judiciary." He denied that the framers of the federal Constitution contemplated or desired judicial review of legislative acts. The judiciary, according to Doster, was subordinate to the branch of government directly representing the popular will:

> As a depository of delegated authority, the Legislature is the only logical and necessary provision of nature in its bearing upon the government of men. All other powers are of secondary delegation from it. Governors and judges are but creatures of legislative fashioning and executioners of legislative will. In a social economy determined upon principles of natural law there is no provision for executive and judicial office. It is only because municipal law cannot be made self-executing—only because the subjects of municipal law do not always yield that ready obedience necessary to an orderly social state—that the legislative will must needs create an agency for its vindication; and this is all it does create, and these are all the powers that do exist—legislative and executive. Among the divisions of government, analytically considered, there is no such thing as judicial power. What we call by that name is merely a function of executive power.[2]

He voiced similar statements in his decision *In re Greer*. Although there were instances of unconstitutional interference with the courts by legislative bodies which should be resisted by the judiciary, the electorate and not the courts was the soundest bulwark against legislative folly and tyranny: "Should the legislature commit any wanton and unreasonable exercise of its authority to regulate the jurisdiction of the courts, the people will promptly rebuke the outrage and command the restoration of power. Happily, therefore, there is no ground for the indulgence of a pessimistic fear of danger to the political system through assaults thereon by the popular branch. Rather, in the opinion of the writer, is the danger to be feared from the exercise of an excess of authority by the courts themselves."[3]

One of the more important cases coming before the court during Doster's term was *State* v. *Haun*. In 1899, Kansas coal-mine operators challenged state legislation limiting their right to issue scrip in lieu of wages and forbidding them to require employees to trade at company stores. Republican justices Smith and Johnston ruled in favor of the operators, holding that the statute in question was unconstitutional because it amended corporation charters without so indicating in the title of the act. It was invalid also because of a provision limiting the scope of the law to corporations employing ten or more workers; this, they wrote, was a denial of equal protection of the laws as guaranteed by the Fourteenth Amendment. Doster dissented, arguing that the title of a law amending a corporate charter need not indicate the fact in so many words. He also denied that the law was discriminatory. Once again he made a plea for restraint: "It is a fundamental rule of a judicial action to resolve all reasonable doubts as to the constitutional validity of a legislative enactment in favor of the statute."[4]

In another case involving the state's attempt to regulate the mining of coal, Doster's views were again on the side of reform. In 1893 the legislature passed a "screen law" which compelled operators to pay the miners on the basis of the gross amount mined. Johnston joined in an opinion upholding the law's constitutionality. Doster and Johnston held that it was a proper exercise of the police power. It was, moreover, beneficial in that it would lead to better accounting practices which in turn would give statistics on which to base bargaining for wages. The statistics, they believed, would also benefit the consumers. In dissent, Smith wrote that the majority view distorted the intent of the law's framers, who had wanted to regulate wages, not produce statistics.[5]

Doster disagreed with Johnston and Smith when, in *Evans* v.

Kahn, they implied that a mortgage was a title to land rather than a security. The Chief Justice charged his colleagues with reviving an old common-law concept long since abandoned. He argued that a mortgage, under recent rulings, was merely a security and to treat it as an instrument of title was to revive the old concept as a legal fiction.[6]

In a case concerned with the validity of an act allowing the voters of Douglas County to establish a court by referendum, Doster joined Smith and Johnston in nullifying the law because certain of its sections were not in harmony one with another. He took the occasion, however, to write a separate opinion in which he upheld the desirability of direct democracy: "The writer, speaking for himself alone, is firmly of the opinion that the principle of direct legislation is the wiser and more democratic principle and would like to see it incorporated into the political system of the country."[7]

When the Republicans regained control of the state in 1898, one of their first actions was to remove the Populist regents of the Kansas State Agricultural College on the charge of misconduct. Their removal was appealed to the Supreme Court. Johnston and Smith ruled that the administration was within its rights. The Chief Justice wrote a scathing dissent. The college, under President Thomas Will, had been a Populist stronghold, and to Doster the ousting of the regents was a palpable effort to remove Populistic influences. He considered the charges "trivial" and "conceived and prosecuted in that spirit of malignant partisanship which is the curse of American politics." He closed by saying: "Similar charges and proceedings by the office-seekers of my party will never have countenance by me, nor will I be deterred from denouncing those made and conducted by political opponents as causeless, wicked and despicable."[8]

Another successful effort by the Republicans to uproot Populism culminated in a decision declaring the Court of Visitation unconstitutional. The Court of Visitation, established during the Leedy administration, was a regulatory body designed to exercise closer control over the railroads and to set rates. The Republican justices ruled that the new agency "commingled" executive, judiciary, and legislative powers. Doster disagreed, arguing that "in the practical affairs of government there is not and cannot be any such thing as a clearly defined and complete separation of powers. . . . The metaphysical distinction between the spheres of will, judgment and action cannot be applied in the domain of political science." The railroads were too complex to allow ordinary courts to regulate rates. Special tribunals were needed. "To refer an aggrieved shipper to the common-law remedy is like holding the word of promise to the ear and breaking it to the hope." Harking back to the touchstone of his political philosophy, Doster declared that "The business of railroad transportation is of vital public concern. It is clothed with a public interest. It is not *juris privati*. That was decided in the case of *Munn* v. *Illinois* . . . and has been repeated in a multitude of decisions since that one was made." In another dissenting opinion he cited Sir Matthew Hale to support his view that a common carrier was "clothed with a public interest."[9]

Another Populist statute, an antitrust law of 1897, was challenged on the basis of rulings of the United States Supreme Court which held that similar acts were invalid because they could be construed to be operative against village grocers and farmers. Doster seized the opportunity to take issue with such reasoning. The intent of the framers was clearly to do away with "gigantic combinations of capitalistic interests, having for their object the suppression of competition, the control of prices and monopolization of markets." He was careful to say that he was not necessarily defending the need for these laws; he was only pointing out that legislators were acting on the widespread demands for such legislation. The laws were designed to apply to large corporations only. "How vain, then, to affect to find the small personal affairs of obscure and irresponsible individuals, totally lacking all the elements of public concern, embraced within the legislative cognizance and made the subject of hostile legislative fiat." Furthermore, it was unnecessary "to launch the platitudes of personal liberty and freedom of contract and due process of law, etc., against the statute. What specific prohibition does it contain that the common law has not contained for ages past? Absolutely none." In this decision, delivered in 1902, Doster spoke for five of the six Republican justices as well.[10]

In an earlier opinion he voiced his disagreement with the "exaggerated extent to which the supremacy of the Federal Constituton and law of the affairs of states has been carried." He believed that "many refinements of construction have been placed upon the Fourteenth Amendment to adapt it to purposes not within its original intent."[11]

Doster's opinions, particularly those of the earlier years of his term, warmed the hearts of his Populist admirers. His dissenting opinion in the Davis case, involving an alleged bribery attempt by a Republican, was especially popular with members of his party. State Representative Edward Jaquins of Cowley County hailed Doster as "the greatest man in the Southwest": "He is unquestionably, by reason of that decision, the hero of the hour. He is the greatest man in Kansas. He uttered sentiments which are in full accord with the ideas of the people. . . . Doster's opinion is for the people."[12]

The Populist Chief Justice seldom, however, used his judicial opinions as a means of advancing ideas he held, or was believed to hold, on social questions. A case coming before the court in 1898 involved the right of a woman to leave a bequest to a Catholic priest for her redemption from purgatory. The plaintiff contested the will, claiming that the common law forbade bequests for "superstitious" purposes. Doster, the supposed "atheist," held that only that part of the English common law applicable to America was adopted in the United States and rulings made during the Tudor and Stuart periods could not be countenanced when repugnant to American concepts of religious toleration. "We may question the soundness of her belief, and may deride the claim of efficacy of the service she desired to have performed, but the law has no care for contrariety of faith as to spiritual things, and will, therefore sanction the bequest she has made."[13]

The crusade for women's rights had no stronger champion in Kansas than Judge Frank Doster, but in one of his decisions he acknowledged that the rights of men and women were not the same. "Say what we may in advocacy of the civil and political equality of the sexes, there are conditions of inequality between them, in other respects, which the law recognizes, and out of which grow differing rights and liabilities."[14]

In *Anthony* v. *Norton,* the alleged "free-lover" came down hard on seducers of women. His decision upheld the ruling of a lower court awarding damages to the parents, even though the woman involved was twenty-five years old. "There is no magic in the passing of a daughter's eighteenth birthday anniversary to relieve against parental solicitude and care, or parental anguish over her fall from virtue. At what time in the advancing age of a daughter the feelings of parental mortification over such fall become sufficiently dulled and the sense of parental responsibility sufficiently weakened to reduce the damages to a nominal sum or to deny them altogether we need not concern ourselves."[15]

Doster delivered two important decisions highly favorable to the railroads. His opinion in *Atchison, Topeka and Santa Fe Railway Company* v. *Willey* established the "stop, look, and listen" rule in Kansas.[16] The principle, when adhered to rigidly, makes it virtually impossible to recover damages from the railroads when trains collide with vehicles and persons. In *Railway Co.* v. *Campbell* Doster reiterated his belief that "a strained and artificial construction" had often been placed on the due-process clause of the Fourteenth Amendment, but joined his Republican colleagues in declaring unconstitutional a Populist enactment requiring railroads to issue free passes to shippers of stock. Even though he believed in the reserved power of the legislature to amend corporate charters, he held that the law in question operated as a "substantial impairment" of the "vested rights" of the railway companies.[17]

As a justice of the Kansas Supreme Court, Doster was precisely the upholder of the common-law tradition that he claimed to be. Only when some of the important reform measures enacted by the Populists were questioned did he appear to be partisan. Even in these cases his views were not appreciably radical, and he was usually able to muster an impressive body of precedent to support his opinions. Then too, the Republican members of the court were often in agreement with him since he was not noticeably radical, and they were by no means reactionary.

In nonofficial utterances, however, he was as ready as always to play the Jacobin. Shortly after his election in 1896, he told a reporter: "I don't believe in hell fire, nor human slavery, nor the gold standard, nor in millionaires, nor in the wage system. I do believe in the Ten Commandments and the Golden Rule, in the initiative and referendum, and evolution and woman suffrage and I am edging toward theosophy and Christian Science, and open to conviction in favor of any vagrant fad that nobody will admit believing in until enough do to make it respectable." He claimed boldly that he had been "an adherent of socialism all [his] life." Socialism, he informed the public, was going to be established through the socialization of public utilities. "If you live to a good old age, you will wake up to find yourself living in an almost communistic society, having gotten there by transitions so easy and natural you didn't realize their occurrence until the job was done."[18]

Doster's remarks on socialism in this instance drew the anger not of the local press, but of a New York socialist publication, *The People*. In an article entitled "Raising Dust," *The People* tore into the statements of the Kansas jurist for "their tergiversation, their duplicity and their ignorance." Doster had defined socialism as "the faith or doctrine of those who would organize society upon a more fraternal and co-operative basis." This, according to the socialist journal, "is the definition of a scuttle fish, it is the definition of a political crook, who, wanting a job, spreads his sails to every wind, is everything to every man, and is too cowardly to express a manly opinion, if he has one." The Kansas proletariat, said *The People*, must turn from the Populist tools of the silver-mine barons and support the Socialist Labor party "which will stand out for socialism clear as a pike—the Doster dust notwithstanding."[19]

Whatever the objections of the New York socialists to him, Doster was still one of the darlings of the local radicals. At a meeting of Topeka's Social Democrats of America, he called for the abolition of debt:

It is the most universal, most persuasive system of servitude that the world has ever known. It seems to have never occurred to us to rise against the claimed right of the banker and usurer to divert the medium of exchange from its proper use. Rarely has anyone openly said that money has no proper power to increase. As early as possible this truth must be insisted upon;—that man must be emancipated from the principle of debt, that man must be prohibited from entering upon this immoral obligation. The institution of debt must and will some day be abolished.[20]

In 1897 he wrote to former Populist Lieutenant Governor Percy Daniels and expressed his concern over the widening gap between the country's millionaires and the poor. "I have come to the conclusion that the saving grace in social life is the democratic sense of equality. Inequalities of moneyed fortune such as exist between Rockefeller and the common laborer are as abhorrent as the inequalities in political station such as exist between a monarch and his vassal. The one form of inequality will be tolerated no more than the other." That same year he signed a petition to the Kansas Legislature protesting the invalidation of the income-tax law by the federal Supreme Court.[21]

In his own affairs, however, the Chief Justice was still a small-town property owner, selling and collecting rent from his town lots and farm lands in Marion County. His agent in Marion kept him abreast of his efforts to collect on rental properties, promising to "go after" one of Doster's tenants if he did not pay soon.[22]

During his term Doster lent strong support to at least one concrete reform. In 1900 a proposed amendment was placed on the ballot which would do away with the Courts of Appeal and increase the number of Supreme Court justices from three to seven. The Courts of Appeal, established in 1895, were the highest courts for misdemeanors and civil cases involving less than two thousand dollars. Doster publicly endorsed the abolition of the appellate courts because he believed the system to be blatant class discrimination. Every citizen, he maintained, should have access to the state's highest tribunal.

> Under the present system this right is denied to him unless he is rich enough to have a two thousand dollar lawsuit, or unless he is accused of one of the graver crimes. . . . Two hundred dollars is as much to many men as two thousand or even two hundred thousand to others, and a sentence of six months jail confinement may be as unjust to one man as a sentence of six years confinement in the penitentiary may be to another. A judicial system which provides a high court for a wealthy litigant or a great rogue, and a lower court for the humbler suitor or petty offender, is undemocratic, is in fact monarchical in its spirit and plan, is unjust and ought not to be allowed.[23]

Like most Americans, Doster was shocked at the assassination of President McKinley. Addressing a Topeka memorial service, he called the late president a "clean, decent, moral gentleman"; but his main theme was a denunciation of the treatment alleged to be given to the assassin. "I protest against the barbarous torture, unheard of since the Dark Ages, said to be inflicted upon the miserable wretch to extort from him unwilling and perhaps perjured confessions."[24] Doster likewise extended his compassion to a less well-known murderer. Albert Denham, a McPherson county hired hand, in an attempt to kill a farmer who had slandered him, killed the man's wife instead. Doster, acting as a private citizen, exerted his influence in an effort to persuade Governor William E. Stanley to grant a conditional pardon. Denham, said Doster, had had "much provocation" since his intended victim had ruined his reputation and had succeeded in having him disinherited.[25]

Whatever his humane feelings for murderers, Doster was

as much a militarist as ever. At the close of the Spanish-American war he lauded the "fratricidal strife" which had been "the delight and desire of man" in all ages. "It seems to be God's plan for the working out of the redemption of the race. It would seem to be the evolutionary process by which we mount into the higher realms of being for the cleansing and purifying of the Kingdoms and governments of men."[26]

The war against Spain had an enthusiastic supporter in the Chief Justice of Kansas. During the conflict (in which his eldest son Chase served) he visited Camps Alger and Thomas. He spoke out angrily against the sensational press then spreading stories about unsanitary conditions at the two posts. He defended Republican Secretary of War Alger and called criticism of his administration of the camps "contemptible."[27]

As was true of so many Populists and Democrats, he supported the war but was adamant in his opposition to the seizure of Puerto Rico and the Philippines. Speaking at the Bryan notification meeting in August of 1900, Doster told the audience that the imperialistic policy of the Republicans was absolutely contradictory to the Declaration of Independence and the Constitution. The theory of government by the consent of the governed could not be "taken only in a limited and qualified sense." Self-government did not mean "self-government subject to the control of such so-called superior race or nation as chooses to exercise sovereignty and guardianship over the people." Denying the rights of the Constitution to the new dependencies was "the infamous doctrine of George III, reasserted over again and applied to American soil and American citizenship, and the reason for asserting it over again is that the power of official rule and the power of wealth may have the opportunity to exploit themselves in schemes of imperial empire and consume the substance of a weak and defenseless people."[28]

Doster's views on imperialism reached a national audience when he published an article, "Will the Philippines Pay?" in the May, 1901, issue of *The Arena*. He began by announcing that he would not touch upon the moral aspects of imperialism but rather its supposed profitability: "I shall talk about dollars." In the first place, the colonial experience of Holland and Great Britain showed that white men did not thrive or settle extensively in tropical areas. "No white man can live in a land where the people pick their breakfast off trees" without losing "the characteristics that have made the white man a factor in the world's progress." In addition, the habits and needs of tropical peoples precluded extensive trade with more developed countries. "The conception of a Malay at the equator loading up his larder with American flour and canvassed hams, and his wardrobe with woolen underwear or imported cotton, or storing his tool-house with sulky-riding plows, self-binders and steam threshers, is the conception of Capricorn and Cancer obliterated—a thing impossible to the dream of any but the market-mad commercialists of this age." Nor did Americans need the produce of the islands: "there is not a product of forest, mine or soil in the Philippine Archipelago that does not also lie within three days' voyage from our own shores, ready at hand for the reaching out and taking." And it was not necessary to possess a country in order to trade with its inhabitants: "Trade does not follow the flag. It follows the best bargains or inducements."

Next Doster cited government statistics to show that *"the profits on our Philippine trade for the next two hundred years could not give us back the money thus far expended in the* [suppression of the Philippine Insurrection] *with a reasonable rate of interest on the amount.*" The Philippines, then, would not pay the American people as a whole and it was "opaque, impenetrable, pitiable" idiocy to think that it could. He closed, however, by hinting darkly that a few "syndicates, landgrubbers, and exploiters of the labor there" would realize handsome profits.[29]

As a public figure, Doster was called upon for his views on Kansas affairs. In 1900 the publisher of the Topeka *Capital* invited Charles M. Sheldon, the renowned minister of Topeka's Central Congregational Church and author of *In His Steps,* to edit the *Capital* for a week "as Jesus would." When asked for his opinion of the first issue, Judge Doster replied that he approved of the experiment because it was teaching the public "to value a cleaner journalism free from libel, extreme partisanship, questionable kinds of advertising and editorial and reportorial lying." Doster regretted, however, that the Christian daily had "too much of the characteristics of [a] Sunday school paper": "It will not be a success in any respect if given over to advocacy of Sabbath observance and temperance crusades."[30]

A local periodical calling itself *The Kansas Knocker: A Journal for Cranks* invited prominent men of the state to give vent to their pet dislikes. The July, 1900, issue featured a piece by Chief Justice Doster. In it he revealed a hitherto little-known characteristic, a sense of humor—albeit a caustic one.

He began by announcing: "I am a knocker by instinct, and professionally. I am not satisfied with things. I don't like the existing order. Give me the raw material to work with and I can make a great deal better world than this." He would, like Robert Ingersoll, "make health catching instead of disease." He wanted also to make "good sense, good manners, good looks and other virtues epidemic instead of exceptional."

Then Doster singled out the first object of his wrath: the college student. He would "reform him or kill him off." "I know we pretend to dote on him, and affect to believe that he is the hope and first care of the state, but it's a lie. We don't. Nobody but his mother does."

> Why do I say these hard things about him? I say it because he is self important, noisy, conceited, ignorant of practical wisdom, parts his hair in the middle, flaunts his fraternity badge and school colors in an offensive, challenging sort of way in everybody's face, and prances up [the] street yawping his ear-splitting college yell to the fright and disgust of all timid, sensitive folk within sound. I saw him at the Twentieth Kansas reception . . . making more noise and taking up more room than the whole procession, elbowing everybody out of the way, and drowning the voice of the orators and the music of the bands with his idiotic "Rock Chalk Jay Hawk, Rah Rah Rah Washburn, rah Baker, hurrah! or whatever the infernal Siwash gibberish is.

Doster concluded his diatribe against the student by writing that "I . . . think he takes up too much room, and makes too much noise, and costs too much money, and is too smart in the budding days of his career. If he could only be induced to subside somewhat, to practice a little the modest habit of self-effacement, go out and soak his head, turn an X-ray upon his inwards and see himself as others see him, we could possibly endure him instead of filling up with wicked wishes for his assassination. But he won't."

Worse than the college student, however, was the old man who wanted to go to war. Recruiting officers for the recent war "were distracted nearly to suicide by demands for place made by old bald-headed relics of the Mexican and Civil wars, in their lean and slippered pantaloons, sans teeth, sans eyesight, sans sense, sans everything necessary for the arduous duties of a soldier." War was for boys "and nobody but a durned fool boy is fit to have anything to do with it." Doster held up General Joseph Wheeler as the worst of the lot.

> I haven't anything against Joe Wheeler . . . except his pertinacious insistence on considering himself still alive and on earth, instead of dead to all intents and purposes. In his young and ante-billy goat days he was quite a man. He was then able to do things and did them. He captured my overcoat down in Tennessee in the late fall of '64, and left me exposed to the chill winds of the rapidly approaching winter, but I'll forgive him that if he will only abate, subside, cool off, muster himself out, go and marry the widow Childs; anything, in short, that will repress the ribald horse laugh that everybody feels like giving him.[31]

A patriotic reader of Doster's sentiments on Wheeler took offense and believed it to be disgraceful that "one holding such an exalted position . . . could use such language" to describe the old Confederate.[32]

The Chief Justice had become so respected in the eyes of the Topeka community that he was invited to deliver the commencement address for Washburn College in 1901. Following a prayer by the Reverend Charles M. Sheldon, Doster rose to speak. He dwelled largely upon the industrial wonders wrought by the nineteenth century and the promise of the twentieth century. The genius of the Greeks had been beauty; of the Romans, jurisprudence; and of the Jews, ethics and religion. The genius of the present age was commerce. Rather than speak disapprovingly of it, the Populist orator praised its achievements—the multitude of inventions which were rapidly bringing comfort and betterment to the masses. Doster admitted that the industrial age was necessarily one of concentrated capital and huge corporations. He warned, however, that no one man or organization should hoard all the use and benefits of any of the new inventions. The people had a stake in them because they utilized water, air, and the produce of the earth—the common property of all; no man had the right to harness the physical energy of the world for his own profit exclusively. On the contrary, the fruits of industrialism tended to bring equality among men.

> The very forces and agencies through which these wonderful industrial and commercial changes are made, and these wonderful institutions of modern life are built up, are welding and integrating society into conditions of equality and amity. This is so because they deal with the great universal properties of matter and mind, and, because doing so they beget conditions which affect society as a whole. Because they depend for their motive force upon the universal properties of nature they therefore clothe themselves in a garb of public interest and thus become the commercial property of all.

Another characteristic of the age was the urbanization of society. This the former country lawyer accepted without regret or bitterness. Indeed, he told his listeners that they should have little to fear and much to hope for in the twentieth century. He confessed that he was "in love with the spirit of this age":

> Not that it is altogether loveable, not that it is devoid of sordid meanness, because it is not; but because, commercial and materialistic as it is, it is nevertheless a nobler spirit than that of any of the ages past. There is in the world today, as the direct result of its workings, more that ministers to the rational desires and elevates and enlarges the soul of man than there ever was before. Education today is more widely diffused, morals purer, religion more rational, sentiment upon all subjects more tolerant, houses warmer, clothing better, food more palatable and wholesome, labor lighter and yet more effective, government freer, art more beautiful, books more plentiful, social intercourse more constant and congenial, homes happier, health more assured, and withal a wider philanthropy and a more abounding charity. We live today a larger life than ever before, and we live it because the soul has grown big upon the food of those great events which have

taken the form of vast commercial enterprise and socialized industrial effort.

Doster conceded that many of the phenomenal achievements were motivated by a greed and tyranny that could lead to "industrial serfdom" if not checked. Even in such cases, however, the process still led to a concentration of resources which would inevitably result in "the legalized state called collectivism."

In conclusion he directed his remarks to the graduating class:

> The person who sets himself in harmony with the general spirit of the age, who catches its enthusiasm and puts himself under its vitalizing, energizing influence is the one who with others of like temper will mold the policy and shape the destiny of the American people and the world. So I welcome the new invention, the new discovery, the new labor saving device, the new combination, the great new enterprise. I know they can not make the world worse. I believe they can and do make the world better.[33]

The Chief Justice's oration caused no little controversy in the press. If Doster was up to his old trick of making noises for the sake of "stirring up the animals," the speech had the desired effects on the editors of the Topeka *Capital*. The *Capital* praised its optimism but deplored what was interpreted as the Judge's subtle plea for communism. On the other hand, the *Mail and Breeze* (published by young Arthur Capper) believed the speech represented a complete turnabout in Doster's thinking. A cartoon in the June 28 issue gave two views of him. In the first (labeled "Doster in 1892") he is standing on the "Omaha Platform" ranting that "We are on the verge of moral, political and financial ruin." The second portrays "Doster in 1901"—well-dressed, composed, and dignified on the "Washburn College Rostrum" saying: "To-day, morals are purer, religion more rational, houses warmer—clothing better —food more wholesome—homes happier—health more assured—and we live to-day a larger life than ever before."[34]

The Kansas City *Journal* lauded the spirit and literary quality of the address and then warned that it was questionable if Doster had "really reformed from his execrable doctrines of a few years ago." The *Journal* suggested that the change was superficial and influenced by a desire for reelection in the following year.[35]

There was no substantial variation between what Doster told the Washburn graduates of 1901 and that which he had often expressed before. The belief in the inevitability and desirability of concentration and combination was perhaps his most consistent theme. There was now only a more heightened optimism. In retrospect, the "calamity howler" of the gloomy nineties appears to have metamorphized into a twentieth century progressive.

The transition from Populist to progressive was smooth enough, but Doster faced the coming election year as a man without a party, for fusion in 1896 had meant the decline of Populism. After the defeat of the Populists in 1898, Doster's brother-in-law, Populist state chairman Taylor Riddle, announced that "the cause of the common people now depends upon the organization of the Democratic party in Kansas."[36] The People's party limped through the 1900 elections. By 1902 it was clearly not an important element in Kansas politics.

Doster, however, was reluctant to surrender the party to the Democrats. In an interview early in 1902 he said that he was amenable to cooperating with the Democrats and voting their ticket if they remained willing to adopt Populist principles. He believed it was essential that the Democrats embrace the Populist goals of direct legislation and public ownership of public utilities. Citing the proposed Isthmian canal and President Roosevelt's plan for a national system of irrigation as examples of public ownership, Doster urged the Democratic party to support both the principle and the specific programs. Although he announced that he was "disinclined to be a candidate again" and therefore reluctant to speak about party policy, he nevertheless elaborated on what he expected from the Democrats. He did not want a platform devoted to "anathematizing the trusts and the tariff." The trusts, though evil in themselves, "grow into the ripened state of general ownership and cooperation." Protection was desirable for industries needing it, but he agreed with the Democrats that there should be free trade with the new island possessions. Populists should join the Democrats in opposing "congressional government" of the territories which, except for secession, was "the wildest and most dangerous political heresy that was ever preached in this country." The currency problem, according to Doster, was a dead issue. Although the question was settled "perhaps wrongly," the gold standard would be in effect for many years and it was futile to pass resolutions against it.[37]

The fusionists won out in the Democratic convention in May. The delegates voted to allow the Populists to name candidates for lieutenant governor, treasurer, attorney general, superintendent of insurance, congressman-at-large, and three positions on the Supreme Court. At the Populist convention, Doster received his party's nomination for reelection; not for a full term, but for an unexpired four-year term to fill the vacancy caused by the death of Justice Ellis.[38]

Strangely enough, certain prominent Republicans and Cleveland Democrats showed more enthusiasm for seeing him returned to the bench than many Populists. The Kansas City

Star declared that "if the lawyers whose names appear the most frequently in the docket of the supreme court could have their way there is no doubt that they would re-elect Chief Justice Frank Doster by the unanimous consent of all parties. . . . No judge was more impartial, and to the corporation and the humblest citizen alike he has given equal and exact justice." A lawyer, describing himself as a "Democrat of the Cleveland faith," believed that "Doster the Populist, or Socialist, whatever he may be classed, is one of the fairest men and one of the best judges I have ever found on a supreme bench. . . . He is a credit to the state, a credit to the bench, a credit to his profession." There was a strong movement initiated by the lawyers at the Republican convention to make no nomintion against Doster. The general attorney for the Santa Fe, A. A. Hard, informed the newspapers that lawyers were arriving in large numbers with the object of pressuring the convention into letting Doster be reelected by default. Republican boss Cy Leland was also said to be in favor of the idea. National committeeman D. W. Mulvane publicly stated that if there could be "almost unanimous approval" the place would be left blank on the Republican ballot.[39]

Doster's most vocal support in the Republican ranks came from a Negro newspaper, the Topeka *Plaindealer*. In a special issue the editors urged the Republican central committee to endorse the incumbent Chief Justice:

> He is fair, impartial, a jurist and an educated gentleman. Frank Doster is the choice of the people irrespective of creed, color or politics. Our party did him an injustice in 1896 by saying every mean thing we could about him. We were wrong; let us repent by proving to the people of Kansas that we are for them, that we are not selfish, by endorsing a just man like Frank Doster. Let our committee be broad in this matter and act for our people.

> Politics should not enter such places as the Supreme Bench, and if we do this it will be an example for the whole world. Kansas always leads in the advancement of justice and right, and we should not forsake our duty in this matter.

A case was then pending in the courts involving the right of Topeka's Board of Education to segregate the city's elementary schools. Perhaps the *Plaindealer* supported him in hopes that he would be sympathetic to the cause of integration. The case did not appear before the state's Supreme Court until April of 1903; Doster left the bench in January. It is tempting, yet fruitless, to conjecture about his views on the case. The court, without Doster, decided unanimously in favor of the Board of Education.[40]

Despite the attempt by some members of the party to allow him to be reelected, the Republican convention nominated Rousseau A. Burch as a candidate to oppose him. Had the Republican pro-Doster movement succeeded, reelection would have been certain. Topeka *Capital* writer Jay E. House believed that the Republican Doster boom failed because the Chief Justice was loath to take a hand. House quoted him as telling a friend that "I'd like the compliment and the implied confidence the Republican party would show by nominating no candidate to run against me, but I can't ask them to do it. I can't set the things in motion that might bring it about. I don't know how, and I couldn't do it if I did."[41]

Without the blessing of the powerful Republican party, his defeat was inevitable. Doster, along with other Democratic and Populist candidates, carried only a few far-western counties in the November election. He lost to Burch, 158,323 to 117,272.[42]

There was little rejoicing over Doster's defeat. A Democratic paper, the Topeka *Herald,* commented that "There must be a heap of satisfaction to the Populist party, now that its wild career is closed and it has passed into history, that with all the evils it brought upon Kansas and with all its mistakes and errors, it has to its everlasting credit the record which Chief Justice Doster has made in the Supreme Court. . . . The retirement of Judge Doster is an acknowledged loss to Kansas. The Supreme Court suffers more than the judge in the severance of ties between them." Upon his retirement, the state commissioned George M. Stone to paint the former Chief Justice's portrait which was to hang in the chamber of the Supreme Court.[43]

Columnist House of the *Capital* provided a sympathetic article on the Judge upon the occasion of his leaving office. In appearance, Doster had "the bloodless face, the skin tint of the man who pecks away with mortar and pestle in a busy pharmacy." Nine months out of the year he wore a straw hat "that looks like a part of the crop of 1887." For the winter months he wore a black slouch hat "apparently a relic of a closing out sale at a racket store. His expenditures for personal adornment probably do not exceed $3.65 a year, taking one year with another." House noted Doster's eccentric manner and habits. He was uniformly courteous to either sex but never lifted his hat to women. Being fond of poetry, he always carried verses clipped from magazines and newspapers. An "inveterate smoker," he had purchased the same brand of cigars from the same store in Marion for twenty years; and he never missed a circus.

House entitled his piece "The Retiring Chief Justice of Kansas" and "retiring" meant not only that Doster was leaving the bench but also that he was reticent in the extreme. The writer claimed to have lived under the same roof with Doster for several months but had never exchanged a word with him.

In Marion he had been "as much a stranger to the town drug store crowd . . . as were the men who passed through." Doster was quoted as having said "I'd like to be a good fellow. But somehow I can't learn it. I feel out of place when I work into the scheme in its broader sense." House observed that even the most casual study of the man revealed that "his whole life has been rounded to the home circle" and that the "pride and love for his family has been his incentive and his greatest comfort."[44]

Political defeat did not mean an ignominious return to Marion and obscurity. Immediately after the election the astonishing news broke that the old Populist was to remain in Topeka and succeed Judge Albert H. Horton as assistant general attorney for the Missouri Pacific railroad. The arrangement was believed to have been engineered by the dying Horton and the railroad's general attorney, Bailie P. Waggener. Waggener and his partner James W. Orr were prominent arch-Bourbons in the Kansas Democracy. The newspapers suggested that the move had been under way well before the 1902 election. Certainly Doster had had no intention of returning to Marion even if defeated, for the deed records of Marion County show that the Judge and his wife sold their town property in September and October of 1902.[45]

The Republican papers interpreted the announcement as the "finishing blow to Populism in Kansas." The Kansas City *Journal* reported that "Mr. [George] Gould is fully assured that [Doster] will serve the interests of the Missouri Pacific to the utmost of his ability." The *Journal* was not certain if Doster was prepared to give up his socialistic views, but it predicted that there would be less talk about the rights of the users and fewer outcries over the "bandits" operating the railroads. The same article made the perceptive observation that it was not Doster that had changed, but the public mood:

> Seven or eight years ago Judge Doster would have been denounced as a Benedict Arnold, as a betrayer of the great common people. The Populist newspapers and the Populist orators would have held him up to scorn with the charge that he had sold his principles. And the Judge Doster of that day would scarcely have had the courage to brave the radicalism of his party by engaging himself as an attorney to a great corporation. But such of the Populist newspapers as have mentioned the step of the judge from the supreme bench to the office of a railroad company did so in congratulatory phrases. It does not appear unnatural to them that he should take the best position offered in the line of his profession. . . . It shows, as perhaps nothing else could show, how the fanaticism of Populism has abated and how little present sentiment there is for the strenuous political teachings of a few years ago.[46]

From his retirement from the court until the dissolution of the firm of Waggener, Doster and Orr in 1907, the former Chief Justice labored for the Gould line. His only activities other than his practice were closely tied to his profession. From 1903 until 1905 he was a lecturer on wills and administration of estates at the Washburn College school of law. In 1903 he delivered an address before the Kansas State Bankers' Association on "Legal Phases of Banking." In the same year he declined the office of arbitrator for labor disputes in the coal-mining region of Kansas. He expressed his regrets, saying, however, that he was in favor of the practice of arbitrating differences between capital and labor.[47]

He appeared to be politically indifferent. In the summer of 1903 he announced: "I am not in politics any more. . . . If the Populists have a party in Kansas I will probably be in it. But I am not in politics."[48]

That fall, however, Doster made another stunning pronouncement: he favored Grover Cleveland over Roosevelt for the presidency. He was careful to explain that he was "not a Cleveland Democrat or a Cleveland anything"; but to Doster, Roosevelt was a greater enemy of reform than the New York Democrat. "Roosevelt does nothing except stir up trouble and then go off and leave it." Bryan Democrats and western reformers could expect nothing from Cleveland, but another Cleveland administration would be preferable to living "on a volcano of eccentricity for four years more." Doster went on to blast Republicanism and gave every indication of having found a new political home in the Bryan wing of the Democratic party. Only "a slight difference in tariff schedules" separated Republicans from eastern Democrats. As for the Negro question, the Democrats at least had the virtues of honesty and consistency. They had never pretended to be the friends of the black man, whereas the Republicans sought his favor at election time and for the "balance of the year they lynch him, ostracize him, treat him as a menial, exclude him from white churches and white schools and white recognition just as the South does." Republican politicians never tried to teach the Negro morality, industry, and good citizenship, "or laid before him the fact that he stands in any relationship to society except mere voting relations."

Doster gave his opposition to imperialism as the main reason for preferring the Democratic party. The Republican policy was one of "territorial conquest and colonial government with the incidents of big army and navy, and Caesarism and buccaneering and hell generally." It was hypocrisy to assert that the seizure of the Philippines was justified in terms of Christian obligation. Dollars, not duty, motivated imperialism. "The result has been nothing except a seat at the gambling table of Asiatic politics, and at least ½ billion dollars of money and 25,000 lives lost and more to follow." The catch phrases justifying expansion—"strenuous life," "manifest destiny," "world power," and "extension of commerce"—showed Roosevelt Republicanism to be "nothing but a firecracker and a brass band" with "mere brag and vainglory" as its stock in trade.[49]

Even in announcing, in effect, that he was deserting the near defunct Populist party for the Democrats, Doster demonstrated that he had lost little of his old reforming spirit. He was also willing to work for tangible reforms. A major scandal in Kansas at the beginning of the twentieth century was the administration of the state-owned lands which were sold to help finance the school system. One odious practice was for purchasers of school lands to forfeit their claim, only to claim title again after a subsequent purchaser entered and improved the lands. The laws governing the sale of the lands were sufficiently confusing and vague as to give these claims some validity. In 1907 a western Kansas legislator approached Doster and Waggener and secured their aid in drawing up a bill to eliminate the abuses and protect the rights of the bona fide settlers. Also, Doster and his former opponent T. F. Garver collaborated in writing a pamphlet designed to show that the proposed legislation was constitutional. The measure passed both houses of the legislature and was signed into law by Doster's former detractor E. W. Hoch, governor of the state.[50]

It is erroneous to think of the Progressive era as a period of urban reform only. Nevertheless, even in agricultural Kansas, many of the proposed reforms involved the municipalities of the state. The winter of 1907 brought much misery to the citizens of Topeka, allegedly because the Consumers' Light, Heat and Power Company had failed to provide adequate gas service. When the city attorney announced in August of the following year that the gas company's franchise could not be revoked because of poor service, the outcry against the company became louder. It was also rumored that the company planned to raise rates. Councilman J. W. F. Hughes (of "legislative war" fame) pushed through a resolution empowering the mayor "to secure another lawyer of recognized ability to render an opinion in the matter." The mayor's choice was Frank Doster. The former Chief Justice stated emphatically that "The acceptance of a franchise . . . constitutes an obligation to deliver the goods." Only defects in the product or unavoidable mechanical failures could absolve the gas company of blame. The city, wrote Doster, was within its rights if it chose to revoke the charter for unsatisfactory service. His old enemy Hughes declared that "Judge Doster is a lawyer of too well known ability and the gas company cannot ignore his able opinion. They will simply sit up and take notice before they attempt to raise the price." The Judge's view was possibly a factor leading the manager of the company to deny the rumored rate increase.[51]

By his own admission, Doster would uphold a cause until it became respectable. In his early career he had been a champion of temperance legislation. After several years of prohibition the majority of the people of Kansas were convinced of the desirability of outlawing the bottle. Before 1909 druggists were permitted to sell liquor for medicinal purposes, but the practice was much abused and the legislature of that year abolished the drugstore permit system. The druggists of Topeka came to Doster for an opinion. He wrote that the new law was a violation of the due-process clause in that it deprived the druggist of part of his source of livelihood: "If it takes a man's business, it takes his property." For the remainder of his life Doster was an outspoken opponent of the prohibitory law.[52]

Woman suffrage, however, was not yet a reality and Doster remained a steadfast friend of the movement. In the election of 1912, the franchise amendment was put before the voters. Doster and his family turned their home into a factory for making buttons, badges, and pennants for the cause. In the past he had loathed wearing such paraphernalia, but now he was seen on the streets of Topeka sporting a votes-for-women badge. At a meeting in another Topeka home he told the men present that it was their duty to vote for the amendment even if their wives did not want the franchise.[53]

In November the amendment passed easily, for Kansas, like the rest of the nation, was experiencing an age of general reform. Republicans, Democrats, and former Populists worked for common goals. In 1904, Doster's long-time foe E. W. Hoch was swept into the governorship on a wave of protest against the Cy Leland–Mort Albaugh "machine." During his administration and those of W. R. Stubbs and Democrat George H. Hodges, Kansas adopted the primary, initiative, and referendum; outlawed the railroad pass system; and enacted a host of other reform measures typical of the period. In the fight against Standard Oil, Governor Hoch advocated the establishment of a state-owned refinery.

Doster and the few former Populists still living found satisfaction in the widespread popularity of reform. In his eulogy of Jerry Simpson, Doster reminded the public that "Sockless Jerry" had been the object of "contempt, ridicule, epithet, and anathema" because he had denounced grafting politicians and the trusts and advocated the socialization of public utilities. In less than a decade Simpson's views were those of most Americans. With the exception of bimetallism, all of his programs were incorporated into the platforms of the two major parties. To a Kansas City *Journal* reporter, Doster snorted that the "monumental imposture of the age" was the political party. This was shown by the "celerity with which politicians change their creeds and the facility with which they seize upon and appropriate for their own the creed of some opposing faction or organization." The Republican insurgents in Kansas were "highway robbers" who had "sandbagged old-time Populists in broad daylight and robbed them of all their issues." He did not condemn them but "marvelled how they could do it without a confession of penitence."[54]

Their former opponents often admitted that the Populists had been right. In an editorial of 1906, William Allen White retracted the sentiments of his "What's the Matter with Kansas." He confessed that in it "great sport was made of a perfectly honest gentleman of unusual legal ability, who happened to be running for chief justice of the supreme court of this state, because he said in effect that 'the rights of the user are paramount to the rights of the owner.'" More recently, White pointed out, Andrew Carnegie had said: "People are partners in every great fortune and that there is no private ownership of anything." Had Carnegie made the statement in 1896 he "would have precipitated a panic or riot or both." In 1896 both White and Carnegie were wrong—"and Judge Doster was right." Doster had been "out too early in the season and his views got frost bitten." "This is a funny world," White reflected. "About all we can do is move with it and grow with it. Those who do not move are dead in the shell. But it is interesting to know how universal is the movement toward the social partnership. Andrew Carnegie, Roosevelt and Judge Doster all are crowded in the same car—going up."[55]

While their erstwhile enemies were recognizing the merits

of the programs of the Populists, some of the old agitators were busy chasing the rewards of the industrial age. In 1908 a group of Denver businessmen promoting the Denver, Laramie and Northwestern Railroad held a banquet honoring a former Populist senator from Kansas, William A. Harris, one of the heaviest investors in their enterprise. The other featured speakers were John Briedenthal and Frank Doster. Doster, who was tending to the legal affairs of the corporation, gave an enthusiastic description of the *"illimitable resources"* along the projected route. "I was thunderstruck. . . . *Riches beyond the dreams of avarice; mineral wealth on the surface of the ground only waiting for transportation facilities to put it on the markets of the world."* He also told his audience of his sizable investment in an Arizona mine. Briedenthal cheerfully admitted that "Some of us, a few years ago, started out with the fool notion that we could lick the combines. Some of us have given it up, and . . . the great theory to be acted upon at this time is, 'If you can not lick them, jine them.' "[56]

Doster remained consistent, however, in his attitude toward his other main interests, the law and the legal profession. At the memorial service for one of his old opponents in the Gunn case, Doster eloquently proclaimed that "There is no profession that can claim such freedom of thought, such tolerance of opinion, such kindness of heart, such warmth of fellowship as the profession of law." He also continued his battle for legal orthodoxy. When the state Supreme Court upheld a decision involving the right of a court to enjoin another from hearing a case, Doster poured out his wrath in an address before the Kansas Bar Association, and again in the presence of the Supreme Court justices. He charged the justices with trying "to unfetter themselves from the hard and fast, though plain and fundamental rules of law, in order to do what they conceive to be the justice of the case." Doster asserted that "the law, administered in accordance with the maxims laid down by its great philosophers and magistrates is a science, leading in almost every instance to an exact measure of justice between man and man." Too often, however, the law was perverted by the "morbid and distempered judge treating with contemptuous disregard its plain, elementary principles and substituting therefor his own vague and nebulous imaginings of the equity and justice of particular cases." He urged his colleagues to return to "the law of the venerable masters"—Hale, Holt, Mansfield, Kent, Story, Parker, and Shaw.[57]

In a speech before the bar association of Oklahoma in 1910, Doster made his strongest plea for judicial restraint. He contended that only the legislative branch was the guardian of popular rights and that attempts by the courts to usurp the lawmaking function led to tyranny. He flatly rejected the concept of judicial review, arguing that it was unknown in the English common law and that it was not accepted or anticipated by the framers of the United States Constitution. Marshall had been within his rights in *Marbury* v. *Madison* because he was preserving the constitutional sphere of the judiciary: "each organ of the government in order to [safeguard] its independence and efficiency must be granted the superior capacity for judging of the fitness of those things which peculiarly belong to it, and it is precisely on that ground that the denial of judicial power to annul legislation can be impregnably rested." The people of a civilized country did not need the courts to protect them from their own agents. When legislatures err "the general intelligence will be quick to discover and the general virtue quick to undo the wrong. To assert otherwise is to deny the adequacy of the collective morals and the collective sense."[58]

Doster was said to have put his objections to wrongheaded judges into even pithier language. The story is told among Marion County lawyers that once, after losing a case, he stormed out of the courtroom, accosted a young attorney, and barked: "Do you know what the law is? The law is the ruling of that last son-of-a-bitch beyond whom there is no appeal!"[59]

His concern for the quality of the judiciary moved him to write insurgent Senator Joseph L. Bristow and denounce the proposed elevation of Judge John Pollock to the circuit court. Doster confessed that he had supported Pollock's appointment to the federal district court because he wanted a young man on the bench. Now, however, he was adamantly opposed to him because he believed Pollock to be arbitrary, unreasonable, and ignorant of the law. He was, according to Doster, also guilty of favoring lawyers who were his "club cronies." A final objection "which I think is a serious one, he is in legal view opposed to the enforcement of all recent remedial legislation which seeks to ease conditions in the industrial and commercial fields." Another conservative aspirant unsuited for the place was Charles Blood Smith, whom Doster described as "a syco-phantic fawner on the rich and powerful" and one whose "strongest supporters will be the railroads, telegraph, and Pull-man Car Company attorneys and officials in New York."[60]

As Doster moved into old age, he became increasingly oc-cupied with a new interest—the history of the state. In the fall of 1912 he returned to Marion to deliver the main address at the first annual Old Settlers' Day celebration. Later that year the State Historical Society appointed him a member of a six-man committee etablished for the purpose of marking out the true route of the Santa Fe Trail. As a lawyer and a veteran who had seen duty on the old trail, he was admirably qualified for the responsibility. At the time, several communities were claiming to be located on the route of the trail and contesting the claims of neighboring towns for the same honor. The committee's task was to search through the records and maps held by the society and interview old soldiers, settlers, freighters, and plainsmen in order to provide an accurate map and report. They submitted their findings to the society in the following year. In 1914 Doster made the principal address at the unveiling of the Santa Fe Trail marker at Tampa, Marion County.[61]

By the time of the First World War most of the old Populists were dead, and the battles of the 1890's were becoming faint memories. Doster was no longer looked upon as a dangerous demogogue. He was an elderly, respected Topeka lawyer. His last attempt to seek political office caused scarcely any unfavorable comment. In 1914 he made a halfhearted bid for the Democratic nomination for United States Senator. Although he had the support of some prominent persons, his leading rivals for the nomination had the backing of more powerful elements in the party. Senator William Thompson supported Congressman George A. Neeley; William F. Sapp was the party's national committeeman; and W. L. ("Iron Jaw") Brown was said to be the favorite of Governor Hodges.[62]

His old Supreme Court colleague Stephen J. Allen rallied to his side. In a letter to the Topeka *Capital* Allen dismissed the other Democratic contenders as mediocrities and urged "informed and intelligent" voters to cast their ballots for Doster in the August primaries. "Kansas needs a big man for this big place and Doster if nominated could be elected. It is doubtful if any of our other candidates for the nomination could be."[63]

At Yates Center, Doster opened his campaign by castigating Thompson and Neeley for creating a federal patronage machine to promote Neeley's candidacy. He hinted that their

147

scheme was being encouraged from Washington. In an interview following the address, however, he denied that he was implicating President Wilson.[64]

As a Democrat, Doster was compelled to reconcile his belief in the necessity of industrial concentration with Woodrow Wilson's New Freedom and the traditional laissez-faire tenets of his party. In a speech at Minneapolis, Kansas, he acknowledged that in the early years of the republic the Democratic party fought for individual liberty and against governmental restraint. In the twentieth century the formation of industrial combines posed a new threat. Using the old slogans of liberty and sanctity of property, the rapacious corporations claimed the rights and privileges belonging to individuals. A Democrat had to realize "that he is now in a fight against industrial tyranny as his father was in a fight against political tyranny." He warned that "Power of whatever kind is always oppressive. That is just as true of industrial power—the power of aggregated wealth to affect the fortunes of men, as it was true of political power—the power to control the actions of man." Doster cautioned his fellow Democrats that they should not make war on big business simply because it was big, "but only because it is sometimes bad." Here his ideas were not in accord with the New Freedom ideology but compatible with the view of Theodore Roosevelt—whom he had professed to despise. Still he believed that the fight against the corporations was consistent with the historic mission of the Democracy, since the battle was for the benefit of the individual.[65]

The Minneapolis speech was Doster's only major campaign effort. His reticence led members of his family to take the initiative. His daughter Irma and the wife of his son Chase made headlines with a novel campaign device. At Emporia they attracted a crowd with Irma's playing of the violin and

Mrs. Doster's singing. After the brief concert Irma launched into a spirited two-minute speech for the Judge. She explained that he was "too modest to get out and talk for himself and we feel that Kansas could never have a better United States Senator than father." The two ladies repeated the performance in a few other towns. His brother-in-law Taylor Riddle published an advertisement assuring his fellow Democrats that "Judge Doster is supported by more big men in the Democratic party than any other candidate." An advertisement signed by W. T. Luce offered "The Viewpoint of a Working Man": "I, in company with a large body of working men who have similar views on economic and political questions, choose Frank Doster, and we have reasons aside from the question of ability. We believe he will, from personal convictions, more nearly represent us than any of the other candidates. And when I say us, I refer to fully 85 per cent of the people of the country."[66]

In the primary, Doster, with only 9,275 votes, ran a poor third behind Neeley (24,312) and Hugh P. Farrelley (21,318). Still he received more votes than Sapp, Brown, and another old Populist, Jerry Botkin. In the general election, standpatter Charles Curtis (who had defeated insurgent Joseph Bristow in the Republican primary) emerged victorious over Neeley and Progressive Victor Murdock. Doster's family and other supporters seem to have taken his campaign more seriously than he. He reported having spent only $376.25 in the canvass, as opposed to Brown's $3,500, Bristow's $3,536.01, and Curtis' $1,946.55. His shyness was also a factor in his poor showing. Columnist Jay E. House wrote that one gentleman said he had been introduced to Doster twenty-eight or thirty times. Surely he had exaggerated, House quipped, for "We have lived in the same town with Judge Doster for thirteen years and have been introduced to him not more than seven or eight times."[67]

A year later Doster retired from the active practice of law and moved to California so that his tubercular daughter Lenore could benefit from a more healthful climate. The Dosters lived in Pasadena until the end of the First World War. It was said that he took an avid interest in the conflict and was in favor of executing the Kaiser. Even in the 1920's, when many liberals were having second thoughts about the war, Doster was convinced that

> Germany under the domination of its Kaiser was a Frankenstein monster that all the evidences convict of having for fifty years prepared for the very assault on mankind it finally committed. Like a lightning flash out of the clear sky it precipitated upon an unprepared and startled world a war of military subjugation. It secretly invented and made use on land and sea of strange and horrible engines of destruction uncountenanced before then in humane warfare. It stood for military autocracy, the subordination of the civil to the military power. It openly proclaimed the abhorrent doctrine that "might makes right," and brazenly flaunted in the face of mankind the egotistic pretention "Germany over all."

Doster was certain that the "Christlike" Eugene V. Debs, to whom he "would yield to no one in [his] love," had made an "intellectual misjudgment" in opposing the war.[68]

Two of Doster's sons served in the army, but it was not until the end of the war that tragedy struck his family. In 1919 the consumptive Lenore died. In the following year an even sadder fate befell one of his sons. Captain Wade Doster, a doctor, remained in the service as a medical officer. His wife died and he took a common-law wife while serving in New Mexico; believing that Wade was deserting her for another woman, the common-law wife shot and killed him. The shooting and subsequent trial caused a sensation in the Kansas press. Doster, then in his seventies, went to New Mexico to assist in the prosecution. After the woman had been found guilty, the aged attorney rose to make an eloquent plea for clemency. The trial judge delivered an equally touching reply in his verdict.

> I know of no appeal that could possibly be made which could prompt this court to take the action it now intends to take other than the plea just made. . . . I have observed the conduct of Judge Doster since this case first came to trial. I cannot forgo expressing admiration for it. He served a long and distinguished term as chief justice of the supreme court of Kansas; he has been a practicing lawyer for 50 years; his conduct displays habits and characteristics which are peculiarly an ornament to the legal profession, and observing him, it is a matter of pride to the profession that he has acted as he has. The court cannot be unmindful of the things he has said, cannot be untouched by the appeal he has made. It is because of this appeal, because of it alone, that the demands of justice are to go, it may be admitted, greatly unsatisfied. The leniency which the father of the deceased in this case has so beautifully and touchingly demanded of the court will be granted.[69]

The sorrowful Doster and his wife returned to Topeka where he resided for the last dozen years of his life. It would have been natural for the aged Populist, wracked by family misfortune and political defeat, to pass the remainder of his life in silence, bitterness, and obscurity; but Frank Doster could not or would not do what was expected. He continued his career as a defender of radical and unpopular causes and became one of the boldest spokesmen for Kansas liberalism in the 1920's.

NOTES

[1]*Biographical Clippings,* D, II (Kansas State Historical Society), p. 221.

[2]58 Kan. 368 (1897).

[3]58 Kan. 268 (1897).

[4]61 Kan. 146 (1899); Domenico Gagliardo, "Some Wage Legislation in Kansas," *Kansas Historical Quarterly,* VIII (November 1939), 394–96.

[5]*State* v. *Wilson,* 61 Kan. 32 (1899).

[6]60 Kan. 719 (1899).

[7]*In re Hendricks,* 60 Kan. 796 (1899).

[8]*Yoe* v. *Hoffman,* 61 Kan. 265 (1899).

[9]*State* v. *Johnson,* 61 Kan. 803 (1900).

[10]*State* v. *Smiley,* 65 Kan. 240 (1902).

[11]*State* v. *Sholl,* 58 Kan. 507 (1897).

[12]Topeka *State Journal,* June 12, 1897.

[13]*Harrison* v. *Brophy,* 58 Kan. 1 (1898).

[14]*Reading Township* v. *Telfer,* 57 Kan. 798 (1897).

[15]60 Kan. 341 (1899).

[16]57 Kan. 764 (1897); 60 Kan. 819 (1899).

[17]61 Kan. 439 (1900).

[18]Kansas City *Journal,* Nov. 26, 1902.

[19]Topeka *Capital,* Aug. 1, 1897.

[20]*Ibid.,* April 25, 1898.

[21]Percy Daniels, *Swollen Fortunes and the Problem of the Unemployed* (Carthage, Mo.: Thompson Co., 1908), pp. 35 and 13.

[22]A. E. Case and Son to Doster, Dec. 15, 1897, March 14, 1898, and April 6, 1899, Case MSs, University of Kansas Library.

[23]Topeka *Capital,* Sept. 23, 1900.

[24]*Shawnee County Clippings,* XX, Kansas State Historical Society, 14.

[25]Kansas City *Journal,* April 26, 1901.

[26]*Ibid.,* June 3, 1900.

[27]Topeka *State Journal,* Sept. 2, 1901; James C. Malin, *A Concern about Humanity: Notes on Reform, 1872–1912, at the National and Kansas Levels of Thought* (Lawrence, Kansas: The Author, 1964), p. 152.

[28]Topeka *State Journal,* Aug. 23, 1900.

[29]*The Arena,* XXV (May, 1901), 465–70.

[30]*Biographical Clippings,* D, II, p. 222.

[31]Frank Doster, "The College Student and the Old Man Who Wants to Go to War," *The Kansas Knocker* (July, 1900), pp. 11–15.

[32]*Biographical Clippings,* D, II, p. 224–25.

[33]Topeka *Capital,* June 13, 1901.

[34]*Ibid.,* June 13 and 14, 1901; *Mail and Breeze,* June 28, 1901.

[35]Kansas City *Journal,* June 14, 1901.

[36]Malin, *A Concern about Humanity,* p. 210.

[37]Topeka *Herald,* Feb. 11, 1902.

[38]Topeka *Capital,* May 22 and 23 and July 8, 1902.

[39]Kansas City *Star,* June 23, 1901, and Sept. 29, 1902.

[40]Topeka *Plaindealer,* Sept. 29, 1902; *Reynolds* v. *Board of Education,* 66 Kan. 672 (1903).

[41]*Biographical Clippings,* D, III, pp. 305–6.

[42]Secretary of State of the State of Kansas, *Thirteenth Biennial Report* (Topeka: 1903), pp. 74–75.

[43]*Biographical Clippings,* D, III, p. 300; Mrs. Ben Hill Doster, *The Doster Genealogy,* (Richmond: The William Byrd Press, 1945), p. 64.

[44]*Biographical Clippings,* D, III, p. 306.

[45]*Ibid.,* p. 307; Topeka *Daily Capital,* Nov. 19, 1902; *Deed Record Book,* 106, Office of the Marion County Register of Deeds, Marion, Kansas, pp. 379–80.

[46]Kansas City *Journal,* Nov. 20, 1902.

[47]Bar Association of the State of Kansas, *Proceedings of the Thirty-sixth Annual Meeting* (Topeka: 1919), p. 14; *Washburn College Catalogue, 1902–1903* (Topeka: 1903), p. 84; *Ibid., 1904–1905* (Topeka: 1905), p. 79; Kansas State Bankers' Association, *Proceedings of the Sixteenth Annual Convention,* (Kansas City: 1903), pp. 118–129; *Biographical Clippings,* D, III, p. 308.

[48]*Biographical Clippings,* D, III, p. 308

[49]Topeka *State Journal,* Nov. 5, 1903; Kansas City *Times,* Nov. 7, 1903.

[50]Attorney General of Kansas, *Fourteenth Biennial Report* (Topeka: 1904), pp. 12–13; William M. Wells, *The Desert's Hidden Wealth* (Los Angeles: The Author, 1934), p. 217; State of Kansas, *Session Laws,* 1907, pp. 538–40.

[51]Topeka *Capital,* Sept. 25 and Oct. 12, 1908.

[52]*Ibid.,* May 19, 1909.

[53]*Ibid.,* Oct. 5 and 20, 1912.

[54]Annie L. Diggs, *The Story of Jerry Simpson* (Wichita: Jane Simpson, 1908), pp. 266–68; Malin, *A Concern about Humanity,* p. 153.

[55]Emporia *Gazette,* Dec. 14, 1906.

[56]*An Evening with Senator W. A. Harris of Kansas at a Banquet in His Honor Given at the Albany Hotel, Denver, Colo., on March 26, 1908* (n.p.: n.d.), pp. 13, 14, and 22.

[57]*William Henry Rossington, In Memoriam* (Topeka: Shawnee County Bar Association, 1908), p. 17; Frank Doster, "An Appeal to the Tavern," in Bar Association of the State of Kansas, *Proceedings of the Twenty-third Annual Meeting* (Topeka: 1906), pp. 179–82.

[58]Frank Doster, *The Constitution and the Courts* (Kansas City: Smith-Grieve Typesetting Co., 1911?), pp. 13, 19, 26–27, 30, and 31.

[59]D. W. Wheeler to the author, September 22, 1966.

[60]Doster to Bristow, December 7, 1911, J. L. Bristow MSs, Manuscripts Division, Kansas State Historical Society.

[61]*Marion County Clippings,* II (Kansas State Historical Society), 63; Kansas State Historical Society, *Eighteenth Biennial Report* (Topeka: 1913), pp. 102 and 107; and *Nineteenth Biennial Report* (Topeka: 1915), p. 104; Irma Doster, *Freedom has a Happy Ring: A Kansas Bulletin for Kansas Schools* (Topeka: Burge Printing Co., 1960), p. 41.

[62]Topeka *Capital,* July 19, 1914.

[63]*Ibid.,* July 6, 1914.

[64]*Ibid.,* July 11, 1914.

[65]*Ibid.,* July 17, 1914.

[66]Kansas City *Star,* July 19, 1914; Topeka *Capital,* July 18, Aug. 2 and 3, 1914.

[67]Secretary of State of the State of Kansas, *Nineteenth Biennial Report* (Topeka: 1914), pp. 16–18; Topeka *Capital,* July 26, 1914.

[68]Walt Markley, *Builders of Topeka* (Topeka: Capper Printing Co., 1934), p. 81; "Eugene V. Debs," undated manuscript address (probably 1926), Doster MSs, University of Kansas Library; Topeka *Capital,* Feb. 26, 1933.

[69]"Report of the Memorial Committee to the Topeka Bar Association in Tribute to Judge Frank Doster," (1933), Thomas Doran MSs, Manuscripts Division, Kansas State Historical Society.

5

GOD'S PLAN FOR LIVING TOGETHER

DOSTER continued to take on new and unpopular causes even in his last years. Although he based his advocacy of the new liberalism on his old beliefs in social and economic evolution and the public interest principle of the Munn decision, he applied them to the changed conditions of the postwar era. He did not simply represent the last gasp of Populism. During the 1920's he championed internationalism, defended Russian communism, and denounced prohibition, child labor, intolerance, fundamentalism, and the union of church and state.

His most conspicuous theme was his old demand for a purer jurisprudence. In letters to the Topeka dailies he urged the public to free itself from the blind acceptance of judicial infallibility; courts, like administrative and legislative bodies, made mistakes. He cited the Dred Scott decision, the perverse interpretations of the Fourteenth Amendment, and instances of judicial partisanship and favortism to corporations. In 1924 he expressed his sympathy with the demand of the La Follette Progressives for the end of judicial nullification of social legislation. He agreed also with the Wisconsin senator's opposition to injunctions in labor disputes. Doster added that although he approved of La Follette's economic views he did not sup-

port him for the presidency because of the senator's opposition
to the war and the League of Nations.[1]

In talks before the bar associations of Topeka, Wichita, and
Kansas City, he castigated the courts for haphazard "expediency" decisions. The United States Supreme Court's *In re
Neagle* decision was a "monstrous perversion of judicial power"
because it allowed the federal marshal who killed the assailant
of Justice Stephen J. Field to go free. Also objectionable was
a ruling which permitted mandatory prayers in the public
schools. Another instance of flagrant disregard of the state
constitution occurred, according to Doster, when the legislature established drainage districts and limited the voters and
officials of the districts to property owners and taxpayers.
Worse still was the refusal of the state's highest tribunal to
invalidate the act. Doster urged his colleagues to join him in
saying to the justices "without any affectation of deference, but
bravely and to their faces: 'Your Honors, that is not the law!' "[2]

In 1921 the state Supreme Court appointed a commission
to revise the statutes of Kansas. Although not a member of
the commission, Doster was invited to contribute to the final
reports of 1922 and 1923. In them he gave his favorable
opinion on the constitutionality of the bill drafted to revise and
amend obsolete statutes and warned the commissioners against
too liberal editing of the old laws.[3]

Doster continued to be active in the state bar association.
In 1928 he served on its committee on the *Kansas Digest*.[4] His
participation on the association's Committee on Americaniza-
tion and Citizenship in the previous year occasioned a mag-
nificent statement in defense of libertarian principles. By 1927
the Ku Klux Klan was dead in Kansas; but postwar nativism
was still in evidence and found expression in the committee's

report. Chairman W. M. Glenn set the tone in his introductory remarks.

> Talk Americanization in all of our talks, think it in our thoughts and act it in our actions. Even if it is not altogether true in all cases we must be imbued with the thoughts that we are citizens of the greatest country in the world; that our citizens have the greatest prosperity and the greatest opportunities; that we have the smartest men and women; that our men are the best looking and our women the prettiest anywhere; that our United States does more for its citizens than any other country in the world does for its citizens; that our citizens have the greatest prosperity and we venerate and reverence our constitution as the greatest political document ever drawn.

Committee member J. S. Dean (whose "damn heart" Doster had threatened to shoot out in 1891) inveighed against the large number of foreign-born who showed no respect for American institutions, whose "mental diet" was the "radical rot" fed by the newspapers of anarchists, communists, socialists, "and other such cattle." Committeeman I. M. Platt concurred with Dean's recognition of the threat to the nation, but suggested that his proposal for a campaign to repatriate the offenders would be "a rather difficult problem."

In the face of such sentiments Frank Strong, professor of law and former Chancellor of the University of Kansas, made a plea for justice, tolerance, and friendship for the immigrants. He also urged that the native-born obey the laws and thereby set an example for the foreign-born. Doster's reply to the nativists was more direct. He bluntly asserted that good citizenship meant more than a knowledge of the citizen's duties; awareness of his rights was more important. Good citizenship, he concluded, "doesn't consist in meaningless hot air mouthing about 'one hundred per cent Americanism,' nor in servile pretensions of obedience to law merely because it is law, but as a beginning lesson it consists in the knowledge that constitutions are not made for the benefit of majorities, but are made as well, if not primarily for the protection of minorities."[5]

During the 1920's some of Doster's thoughts on the law reached the Chief Justice of the United States Supreme Court. In 1922 William H. Taft wrote Doster's old colleague William R. Smith of the Kansas supreme bench, thanking him for sending a copy of Judge Doster's "thoughtful judicial inquiry" which he commended as "written in a fine spirit and full of interesting suggestions and analogies."[6]

As was evident much earlier in his career, Doster was no atheist even though his public utterances showed him to be far from orthodox. As he advanced in years, however, he became active in Unitarian circles in Topeka. Early in the twenties Doster addressed the Unitarians on the question of man's immortality. The religionists, said Doster, avoided inquiry on the eternal life. With scriptural authority to support their belief, they considered further proof unnecessary. Scientists also neglected the problem, believing it to be outside their province because it involved the spiritual, not the material realm. The future life, however, was a scientific question according to Doster. He based a tentative proof of immortality on the physical laws of the conservation of energy and the "correlation of forces." The first principle taught that energy or force was indestructible. If gravity, heat, light, and radioactivity persisted, why could not human consciousness, or life, persist? Life too was a form of energy. The second principle, the correlation of forces, provided order and harmony in the universe. The Creator would not have endowed all men with the desire for the life eternal without the possibility of fulfillment.

"God's law" of the correlation of forces, therefore, "will give [man] an eternal and a better life."[7]

In 1925, at the annual Laymen's Sunday, Doster again spoke to the Unitarians. This time the topic was his belief in Jesus. He confessed to being a "violator, at heart, of every one of his laws, violator, in deed, of many of them, skeptic to all the religions, atheist to all the gods"; yet he would "uncover [his] head to Him as the supreme excellence of the world." Doster dismissed virgin birth, sacrificial atonement, the resurrection, and other supernatural claims in Christian dogma. Early Christians had borrowed them from paganism and they detracted from the true glory of Jesus. The greatest appeal of the religion of Christ was its "responsiveness to the call of the human heart." The mystic religions of the East stressed release from sin through asceticism and "fixity of thought on abstract virtues." The superiority of the teachings of Christ lay in the command to "love thy neighbor as thyself." The emphasis on love, mercy, truth, and goodness made Christianity unique among the world's religions. Doster was convinced of the existence of the historical Jesus, but preferred not to know Him better, for then He would be "familiar and commonplace;" rather he wanted to look upon Him as "the unknowable mystic of the ages."[8]

Doster's interest in religion did not deter him from speaking out against the intrusion of the church into secular affairs. In a letter to the Topeka *Capital* he denounced Sunday observance laws. The basis of Sabbath observance was the belief in a six-day creation, which scientists and even some ministers rejected. "The idea of cherishing the story of a six days creation, giving it the sanctity of a divine revelation and the authority of penal law, after spending millions of dollars to teach its untruth and after everybody of intelligence has rejected it as a childish fable, is not only a paradoxical but a humiliating fact of human psychology." In a public address he voiced his vigorous objections to religious instruction in the public schools and denied that such instruction was necessary for teaching proper conduct; ethics and morals were not dependent upon religious dogma. "Impossible fables" such as the six-day creation and divine inspiration for the writing of the Bible did not build character, scholarship, or spirituality. Organized Christianity, moreover, had always impeded the spread of learning. For proof he pointed first to medieval Catholicism and then to the recent burning of the *Book of Knowledge* by Kansas Protestant fanatics in Jewell County because it discussed evolution. The Jewell County incident was "a sample of what you may expect should the church succeed in its effort to get control of the educational interests of the country. No need to look at the action of the Tennessee anti-evolution mountaineers for evidence of sixteenth century intolerance and attempt[s] to make men good by making them ignorant."[9]

Doster was especially sensitive to assaults on evolutionary theory because he based his views on social, spiritual, and material betterment on the concept of eternal change. He recognized some absolutes—the "timeless verities" such as freedom, mercy, and love—and he acknowledged that truth existed in a "universal cosmic sense." But for the most part he believed that the "truths" men held were ever-changing and relative. Truth consisted "not in the establishment of fact, but in the exclusion of error." All religious creeds, political doctrines, and scientific laws were the "discards of past errors." The world, however, was better for all these transitory truths, "not as arrivals at final truth but as the leaving off of hindering fallacies."

Men must accept change, said Doster, for the grand design

of the universe is constant evolution towards good. This evoluiton was demonstrated by the various stages of society through which mankind had passed: from Java man (who "overcame the female and then slunk away leaving his offspring to the rude and transient care of the mother") to the family, community, tribe, and nation. As society progressed through patriarchal, priestly, feudal, monarchical, and democratic forms, each step brought "more of the essential elements of unity, freedom, and equality." The increased freedom of thought was especially important in the evolutionary process because of the material and social improvements which resulted.

> Freedom of man to think as he would has transformed the domains of science, government, and theology, and has begun to attack the intrenched and fortified field of economics. And what transformations in the man himself since he began to think! He lives now as the high priests and princes did not in older times. He has a clearer eye, a keener mind, a higher conception of the purpose and obligations of life. He sails the seas in a palace and travels the continent in coaches of luxury a mile a minute and flies the air faster than a bird. He sends his thought on a lightning flash around the globe, and in an incomplete experimental way, but one prophetic of future certainty, through the device called television he talks to his friend on the other hemisphere the while looking at him as though face to face; and recently two deaf mutes conversed with each other a mile apart in the finger sign language. He listens to speech and music a thousand miles away. He looks at the stars through infinity of space and analyzes their elements and calculates the speed of their light. He has unseated kings from their thrones and established himself as ruler instead, has abolished slavery the world over, and year by year is emancipating labor from unrequited toil. Of late, more than ever before, he has accelerated his upward way by the development out of his emotional nature of the qualities of sympathy for his fellows and tolerance of their beliefs.

Doster's tone in this address was not entirely optimistic. He expressed his concern for jobless workers, many of whom had been thrown out of work by the very technology he was praising. He rejected the view that the machine which displaced humans was the end product of evolution. "I deny that economic evolution ends there or has in view that purpose. I believe I know . . . such end or purpose is good to the whole of mankind and not alone to those of that class whom gentlemen approvingly term rugged individualists."[10]

Important also to Doster was the unity and fraternity brought about by the process of social evolution. On Memorial Day of 1929 he returned to Marion where in an address to his former townsmen he reiterated his belief that the Civil War was necessary because "God wills that men do not draw apart from one another, but that they draw nearer." Territorial expansion brought a greater degree of democracy. Political fragmentation in Europe sustained monarchy: "Every petty princeling had to be provided with a little bailiwick to rule, to set off in exclusiveness to others of like kind, out of which grew concepts of self interest and differences in language and religion, and these bred rivalries, and wars, and heavy burdens and constant shedding of blood." The opposite was true in the American experience because the policy of expansion resulted in homogeneity and unity. Secession would have Europeanized America politically and retarded democracy. He did not believe that territorial growth in itself was the aim of government. Rather he wanted to show that expansion of national boundaries was "the means by which the spirit of fraternity and good will among men works out the destiny of mankind to dwell together in amity and peace."

In the Marion speech, he took his thinking to its logical conclusion with a full-blown plea for internationalism: "Nations, to play their full part and fulfill their destiny, have got to think big; to think across continents; think in terms of hemispheres; in terms of leagues of nations, and see Tennyson's vision, 'The parliament of man, the federation of the world.' "[11]

It is evident that Doster's thoughts in 1929 were essentially the same as those of his earlier career. He still believed men were destined to achieve unity and that war was often necessary to advance the process. In his last years, however, he stressed brotherhood, peace, and love; the praise of war for its own sake was absent. The Frank Doster of the 1920's was a much mellower man the Populist spellbinder of the 1890's. No longer did associates and opponents find him cold, vindictive, and vicious. Topeka journalist Thomas A. McNeal described Doster in his last years as a man whose expressionless face belied his tolerance, generosity, and humor.[12]

Although he sought no office, he was a steadfast Democrat. When the state's Repblican attorney general charged Democratic Governor Jonathan M. Davis and Bank Commissioner Carl J. Peterson with selling pardons, old Populist A. M. Harvey, Doster, and his partner John Addington served as their counsel at the trials. Davis faced two trials, both of them after he left office, and the juries voted acquittal each time.[13]

Doster was not enough of a loyal partisan to refrain from condemning both parties as nothing more than "commercial syndicates" organized for the monetary advantage of their members. In an address before the Fourth District Federation of Women's Clubs, Doster assailed the Democrats for pretending to be friendly to prohibition. Worse still was the states' rights cry of the Republicans in opposing the child labor amendment. They were deserting the party's traditional hostility to the principle of state's rights in order that "New England with its factory system, New York with its sweat shops,

Pennsylvania with its coal mines, Virginia with its tobacco works, Georgia and the Carolinas with their cotton mills, might hold the tender bodies and youthful minds of children to the bondage of profit making for others." No political party had made America a powerful nation: rather the American genius for good government, operating through individual liberty, had raised the United States to a world power. Doster rejected also the notion of the virtue of the majority. Minority parties, after becoming majorities, had impeded freedom and progress. In the early days of the republic the Democratic party fought for the liberty of the white man and after attaining power it had "steeled its heart against the enormity of the black man's slavery, and, even now yields only a nominal and grudging assent to the constitutional guaranties of the black man's independence and civil equality." Likewise, the Republicans rose from minority status in their fight against slavery only to let both white and black workers become "serfs of an economic mastery as pitiless as that of the slave driver of the South." No political party was capable or courageous enough to embrace more than one idea at one time. Both major parties, for example, resisted woman suffrage when the Populists and Socialists advocated it and adopted it only when it seemed expedient. The aged judge asserted that opposition to social change was futile and told his female audience that, "The freedom of bobbed hair and short skirts is coming in government too, as well as in dress and style."[14]

Late in the decade Doster reached a wider audience for his views. Now that prohibition was a national fact of life, he wrote two articles against it for *Plain Talk,* a liberal journal with nationwide circulation. In both articles he acknowledged that he had voted for it in Kansas in 1880, but pleaded youth and immaturity of judgment. He was not a drinking man, he wrote, and therefore had no personal interest in repeal. Prohibition was "a mere spasmodic craze," the "latest of many recurrent aberrations of like kind." He gave a blanket condemnation of all sumptuary legislation and pointed out the futility of attempts to regulate personal conduct by law. "Moral legislation almost inevitably brings not reform but corruption." To those who said that the drunkard beat his wife and used the children's bread money for liquor, Doster replied that such injuries to other persons were punishable by law. To those who argued that drinking lowered the moral tone of a society, he replied that this was the identical reasoning used by tyrants and priests in suppressing freedom of opinion and religion. His opposition to prohibition, Doster wrote, would be milder had the churches not advocated it. "When it is recalled that the Church has never stood for a big brave principle of human freedom . . . we may well fear it in its avowed and special championship of liquor suppression."[15]

Although Doster was a socialist in theory rather than by political affiliation, his collectivist thinking became more pronounced as he grew older. Upon the death of Eugene V. Debs in 1926, Doster delivered a eulogy to the nation's foremost socialist and reiterated Debs' cry that "the wages system must go."[16] As the Great Depression set in he became even more vocal in his advocacy of a radical change in the economic system. In November of 1931 the Unitarians of Topeka sponsored a forum to discuss the relative merits of communism, socialism, and capitalism. Doster began the series with an exposition of communism. Sociologist C. D. Clark of the University of Kansas offered an explanation of socialism; and a defense of capitalism by D. J. Teviotdale, also from the university, concluded the forum.

True to his old form, Doster began his address with a

startling pronouncement: "I am a communist in economic belief." He then told his listeners that the statement should not set them against him because their notions of communism were probably false. It did not mean the division and equal distribution of the world's produce. Rather it was "a system under which men do not live by economic warfare with one another, but by mutual helpfulness to one another. It means God's plan of living with one another instead of off one another." The simplest way to hasten the realization of the Divine Plan was through socialization of the utilities "clothed with a public interest." "Now," he asked, "tell me what there is in economic life today that is not clothed with a public interest."

In answer to those who believed economic warfare to be man's natural behavior, Doster asserted the contrary, that "the history of mankind is the history of progression towards associated property interest and equality of economic condition." Examples of shared goods and services were public schools, highways, and the postal system. Contrary to the usual assumption, the history of mankind was "the story of common effort to attain the things of common good." Even warfare was a communal undertaking: "it is selfish and competitive strife—still it is not individual effort and the conquerors have communal betterment in view." The foremost modern examples of communism were the business corporations. "It matters not that they are predatory in character and practice. The point is —the individuals composing them have ceased economic strife among themselves, have pooled their property, have united their efforts, have socialized their interests, have communized themselves as it were, and have become, thereby, prophetic of the universal communism to come."

Replying to the argument that communism would destroy incentive, Doster told his audience that the only incentive in capitalism was for selfish or vainglorious ends. Communism, on the other hand, would inspire individual initiative for the benefit of the whole. Even in a capitalistic society, inventors, statesmen, teachers, and philosophers worked without hope of financial or other personal gain. Communism would encourage rather than destroy such initiative.

Attacking capitalism head-on, Doster decried the waste inherent in the system: overproduction; advertising, which added nothing to the value of products yet cost billions; insurance, to protect "against the frauds and felonies of your fellows"; and the expense for police, courts, lawyers, and legislation which existed "merely to safeguard the interests of private property." The old lawyer insisted that "Nearly all the law on the statute books and in the decisions of the courts is law for the purpose of checking, controlling, punishing, the fraudulent and criminal efforts of men to possess themselves of other men's estates. There is scarcely a wickedness in the daily list of crimes but consists in, or can be traced to the desire and effort of men to advantage themselves of other men's property." Both government and the churches, he claimed, existed solely for mitigating the crimes of the other man-made institution, property.

In closing, Doster pleaded with those present to

study whether strife for property gain is really the divinely ordained plan and destiny of the race. Let's quit lying about Russia; quit the unmanly breaking up of little communist children's picnics on the sham pretext to their being plots of treason against the state; quit paying a half million dollars for a ten thousand dollar a year office, expecting to recoup the overpayment by plunder and graft; quit official boodling; quit stealing; quit practicing petty frauds on one another and calling it "business." Let's accept . . . God's plan of living with one another, and not off one another.

The press and public received Doster's call for collectivism without adverse comment. Topekans and other Kansans were willing to tolerate the well-known heterodoxy of an otherwise respectable old man. But when young sociologist C. D. Clark gave what he intended to be an objective analysis of socialism, the newspaper reports gave the impression that he was praising it. The resultant furor nearly cost him his position at the state university.[17]

Doster's "communism" was of course far from Marxist-Leninist orthodoxy. In a 1932 letter to an old comrade of the Populist days, however, he expressed his sympathy with the attempts of the Russian people to establish a society free from "the savage competitive strife we wage." He admitted that the Soviet government was guilty of ruthlessness, but pointed out that democracy and Christianity had also waged war and revolution in gaining acceptance.[18]

Although he condemned capitalism as vicious and outmoded, he confessed in another address that he participated in the system as an unwilling victim, compelled by necessity to operate within the existing economic framework. He did not therefore claim to be any purer than his fellows; he was only perhaps more aware of "the enormity of the frauds and crimes which go to make up the present day economic life."[19]

Doster delivered his last significant address on February 4, 1933, three weeks before his death. The Topeka bar association held a memorial meeting for the recently deceased Patrick Coney, a pension lawyer and old Republican wheelhorse. His passing left Doster as the only Civil War veteran in the association. Having recently risen from a sickbed, the weak and trembling octogenarian began his speech with a few remarks on Coney's career as an attorney. He then moved to an explanation of the Civil War. The war had been waged for the benefit of all mankind because the Union stood for a self-governing republic wherein the people resolved their differences by friendly, democratic means. Secession would have meant the division of the country into hostile factions; it would have been the admission that men could not live together in brotherhood and that the common man was not fit to rule. If secession had been successful it "would have set back the hopes of the common man and lengthened the lease of kings for centuries to come." So far Doster's words were eloquent but familiar. He closed, however, with what may have been a confession about his own fascination with warfare. He was no doubt speaking of himself when he told of "boys like Pat Coney who, moved more by love of adventure and inspired more by the music of the bugle and drum than sober reflection, . . . stayed the baleful retrogression of world thought which the success of the South would have brought about. And it is not strange that in later years when they begin to see the sun go down and the shadows lengthen, a sense of what the war was fought for, and what it meant comes home to them as never before and the cause they served assumes a sacredness of aspect and looms the largest in their memories." So touched were his colleagues that they voted to hang a framed copy of Doster's speech in the county court room.[20]

Although he had retired from active practice well before his death, Doster often served as counsel for those too poor to pay for legal services. He was also active in Topeka's Lincoln Post of the GAR and was its quartermaster until shortly before his death. During the last week of his life, he put aside his usual reticence and, according to a Topeka newspaper, "mingled enthusiastically" at the annual Democratic banquet at the Jayhawk Hotel.[21]

Doster, the last of the important Kansas Populist leaders

still residing in the state, died helping a reform cause. Economic distress struck Kansas and other parts of the agricultural Middle West in advance of the general depression of the 1930's. As the post-war slump set in, the hard-pressed farmers in Doster's old home in Marion County once again found a scapegoat in the Scully leasing system. In 1921 the Scully lessees banded together and threatened a tenants' strike against the policies of Frederick Scully, son and heir of "Lord" William Scully. A protective committee of the tenants' association induced the county's representative in the legislature and the district's state senator to introduce bills protecting their homes, barns, and other buildings from seizure by creditors. The proposals failed in both houses of the legislature.[22]

The worsened conditions of the thirties led the voters of normally Republican Marion County to send John Riddle, a Democrat and the son of Taylor Riddle, to the legislature in 1932. Representatives of the Scully tenants approached Riddle requesting him to introduce legislation to curb the abuses of the system. Riddle assented and sought the aid of his uncle. Doster, then eighty-six years old, lent his enthusiastic support.

The Judge carefully drafted a bill and told his nephew that any amending would ruin its effectiveness. Riddle introduced the bill on January 24, 1933. The House Judiciary Committee was hostile to the measure, but Riddle succeeded in having it re-referred to the more sympathetic Committee on Agriculture which reported it favorably. The House accepted the bill after much effort by Riddle. The Senate passed the measure but only after making changes; the amendments, as Doster had warned, crippled the bill. Nevertheless Riddle moved that the House concur in the changes. On March 15 the act passed, eighty-nine to one, and two days later Governor Alf M. Landon signed it into law.

In its final form, the law began with an enumeration of the abuses of the Scully contracts. The tenants, it read, paid high rents and all taxes and assessments on the land. Unpaid rents and taxes constituted a lien on the crops. The landlord could demand that livestock and machinery be filed as chattel mortgages, and he could obligate tenants to erect buildings and fences. The tenants were responsible for weeding the public roads running through their farms. They were to perform a variety of other duties including ditching, draining, hedge-trimming, and brush-burning or pay a fine to the landlord. The landlord placed restrictions on the types of crops grown. All grain stalks were reserved for the landlord and none could be fed to the tenants' livestock. Finally, the tenants had to agree to waive the benefits of the exemption, valuation, and appraisement laws of the state.

Although the preamble to the law did not mention the Scully holdings by name, it was an almost verbatim recital of the terms of the Scully contract. The remaining parts of the law branded the lease conditions as "variant from the ordinary and generally used and approved rental agreements" and "harsh, burdensome, oppresive, and extortionate in their terms." As amended by the Senate, however, the law concluded with little more than a statement that such leasing practices were "against the public policy of the state." Weak as the anti-Scully law of 1933 was, it had some long-run influence in reforming the Scully contracts.[23]

The author of the original bill did not live to see its passage. While sitting at Riddle's desk in the House chamber on February 24, 1933, Doster suffered a stroke paralyzing his left side. One of the legislators, a physician, tended him until an ambulance arrived. At his home he recovered consciousness and was able to drink a glass of water. Later reports announced that he was comfortable and able to move his left arm and leg again, but at 5:15 on the morning of the 25th, death came to Frank Doster. After lying in state at a Topeka mortuary, the body was cremated in accordance with family custom. There was no public funeral.[24]

After Doster's death, John Riddle told Carrie that he feared the effort expended in preparing the Scully bill had brought on the fatal seizure. The widow replied that the Judge was an old man in his eighties and that there was no more fitting way to end his life than in fathering reform legislation. Carrie survived him by fourteen years, dying in 1947 at nearly one hundred years of age.[25]

The passing of the old Populist evoked much comment from the press and legal profession. The Kansas City *Star,* with more sense of a good story than of accuracy, said that as a district judge and as chief justice he handed down "startling decisions." The same editorial described him as a "natural liberal thinker" who "could not be hampered by precedent or any rule of thumb." A memorial prepared for the Kansas Bar Association was closer to the truth when it gratefully acknowledged that "the passion and radicalism of the Populist crusade never found expression in his decisions. Mindful of his oath, he took his premises from the law as he found it, and his opinions, always models of lucid and logical statement, were the legitimate offspring of that precedent in which resides the certainty of legal rights and legal duties. He knew that a fickle justice was no justice at all." In a similar vein, members of the Topeka bar memorialized: "Notwithstanding Judge Doster's socialistic beliefs, none of his theories ever influenced his decisions. . . . His opinions were always based upon legal principles, fixed by statutes and established by the most sound judicial precedents." A memorial by the Kansas House of Representatives noted that despite his attraction to speculative thought, he was "throughout his life a strict observer of the law."[26]

William Allen White, once his venomous critic, attempted to assess the significance of Doster's career. Forty years ago, wrote White, Doster's statement that the rights of the users were paramount to the rights of the owner was rank socialism.

> Today with certain restrictions this is the doctrine upon which American civilization is based. Under this doctrine the regulation of public utilities has arisen. Under it confiscation by taxation for social purposes has been established, notably in the inheritance and income taxes. Under this doctrine much of the progress that has been made in the world has been achieved. The rights of the user are indeed paramount to the rights of the owner provided the owner is not using his property for the good of society—for the common good, for the best public good.

> Frank Doster's voice was a voice crying in the wilderness. After him came Bryan, came Theodore Roosevelt, came Woodrow Wilson, came the whole liberal movement of this first third of this century. Time and again publicly and privately The Gazette has apologized to Frank Doster for the cruel, unfair and ignorant commentary we made upon him 40 years ago when he was elected to the Kansas supreme court. Now that he is gone it is a comfort that we do not have to say it for the first time over his grave.

Topeka journalist Tom McNeal, in a sympathetic obituary, gently pointed out an obvious characteristic that seems to have escaped so many observers: "It would not be just to say that he delighted in antagonizing prevalent opinion, but he was never deterred from taking the unpopular side."[27]

It is ironical that Doster died while drafting agrarian reform legislation. Although his name is linked with agrarian crusades, he was not primarily concerned with agricultural matters. He began his public career by pushing the herd law through the legislature of 1872 for the benefit of the farmers of Marion County. He died while trying to bring relief to the tenant farmers of the same area sixty years later. But with one other exception, the 1907 school-lands reform law, there is little else to identify him with the problems of rural Kansas. His was primarily the realm of ideas. He was more comfortable dealing with theory and abstractions.

Granted that there are paradoxes and contradictions in all humans, Doster had more than the usual share: a shy, modest man who obviously enjoyed being the center of controversy; a devoted family man who heard critics accuse him of free-love leanings; an advocate of humanitarianism who extolled the virtues of war; an infidel who revered Christ; a firm believer in the necessity of the Civil War because it helped unify mankind according to "God's plan of living together" and yet an opponent of American overseas expansion; a "socialist" and a railroad attorney; a Kansas Democrat who called himself a communist.

The contradiction most noted by contemporaries—the seeming disparity between his radicalism and his devotion to the common-law tradition—is perhaps the most easily resolved. On the one hand he saw the common law as a guarantor of equal justice to all men. Then too he believed that the Munn decision, which recognized the common-law right of the state to regulate commercial enterprises serving the public, was the cornerstone for building a new social order. Regulation, to him, was the surest means of hastening the inexorable collectivization of society.

A final problem: was he a sincere reformer, or was he simply an unfeeling gadfly who espoused the latest reform ideas with the intention of startling his readers and listeners? While it is true that he often appeared to be more interested in radical doctrine than in the immediate alleviation of society's ills, there can be little doubt that the betterment of mankind was an emotional as well as an intellectual commitment for Frank Doster. Genuine sympathy along with a powerful intellect made him a forceful champion of the cause of humanity.

NOTES

[1]Doster to the editor of the Topeka *Capital,* Aug. 13, 1923, and to the editor of the Topeka *State Journal,* Aug. 14, 1924, Doster MSs, University of Kansas Library.

[2]Doster, "Some Bad Decisions," *Kansas City Bar Bulletin* (March, 1925), pp. 4–10; "Address Delivered by Judge Doster before the Topeka Bar Association" (n.d.), Doster MSs; "Address Delivered by Judge Doster before the Bar Association of Wichita, Kansas, on the 20th Day of October, 1928," Doster MSs.

[3]*Report of the Commission to Revise the General Statutes* (Topeka: 1922), pp. 8, 287–93; *Supplement to the Report (December 22) of the Commission to Revise the General Statutes* (Topeka: 1923), pp. 27–29.

[4]*Proceedings, Forty-sixth Annual Meeting, held at Hutchinson, Kansas, November 16–17, 1928,* pp. 55–56.

[5]*Ibid., Forty-fifth Annual Meeting* (1927), pp. 106–14.

[6]Taft to Smith, July 28, 1922, Doster MSs.

[7]Doster, *The Future Life: Address of Frank Doster, Former Chief Justice Supreme Court, Kansas, before the Unitarian Churches of Topeka and Salina, Kansas* (Topeka: ca. 1922), pp. 3–6, 8, 9, 11–13, 16, and 18.

[8]Topeka *Capital,* Dec. 13 and 14, 1925; Doster, "My Belief in Jesus" (1925), Doster MSs.

[9]Doster to the editor of the Topeka *Capital* (n.d.), Doster MSs; "The Law of Religious Instruction in the Public Schools" (1926), Doster MSs.

[10]Doster, "Evolution Makes for Good," undated address, Doster MSs.

[11]Doster, "Memorial Day Address Delivered at Marion, Kansas, May 30, 1929," Doster MSs.

[12]Topeka *Capital,* February 26, 1933.

[13]John W. Ripley, "Chronology of Events—Pertinent and Impertinent —of the Jonathan M. Davis Bribery Trials," *Bulletin of the Shawnee*

County Historical Society (Dec., 1965), pp. 57–59; Topeka *Capital,* Jan. 13 and 23, May 19, 1925.

[14]Doster, "4th Dist. Federation of Womens Clubs. Delivered at Council Grove, Kansas, by Judge Frank Doster 10-21-26," Doster MSs.

[15]Doster, "Prohibition Craze," *Plain Talk* (November, 1927), pp. 27–31; "Kansas Puritanism and Prohibition," *Plain Talk* (July, 1928), pp. 22, 24, and 25.

[16]Doster, "Eugene V. Debs" (1926), Doster MSs.

[17]*University Daily Kansan* (Lawrence), Nov. 16, 1931; Topeka *Capital,* Nov. 1 and 2, 1931; Doster, "Communism—What is it and Why" (1931), Doster MSs. Three letters in the possession of C. D. Clark give the story of his difficulties: E. H. Lindley to Clark, Nov. 16, 1931; C. M. Harger to Clark, Dec. 3, 1931; Clark to Harger, Dec. 10, 1931.

[18]Doster to "Mr. Emmons," June 4, 1932, Doster MSs.

[19]Untitled, undated address, ca. 1925, Doster MSs.

[20]Topeka *Capital,* Feb. 14, 1933; *Journal of the Bar Association of the State of Kansas,* I (May, 1933), 319.

[21]Grand Army of the Republic, Headquarters Department of Kansas, *General Orders No. 5, Wardell Administration, Series 1932–1933* (Topeka: 1933); Topeka *State Journal,* Feb. 25, 1933.

[22]Homer E. Socolofsky, "The Scully Land System in Marion County," *Kansas Historical Quarterly,* XVIII (November, 1950), 350–52.

[23]John H. Riddle to the author, Feb. 4, 1966; *Journal of the House of Representatives, Twenty-eighth Biennial Session, 1933* (Topeka: 1933), pp. 122, 131, 137, 200, 217, 230–31, 635, 645, 656, 666, 695. (Hereafter cited as *House Journal.*); Topeka *Capital,* Feb. 8, 1933; State of Kansas, *Session Laws,* 1933 (Topeka: 1933), pp. 358–59; Socolofsky, "The Scully Land System in Marion County," p. 357.

[24]Topeka *Capital,* Feb. 25 and 26, 1933.

[25]John Riddle to the author, Feb. 4, 1966; Marion *Record-Review,* Jan. 16, 1947.

[26]Kansas City *Star,* Feb. 27, 1933; *Kansas Reports,* CXLIV, iv–v; "Memorial of the Topeka Bar" (1933), Doran MSs; *House Journal,* pp. 775–76.

[27]Emporia *Weekly Gazette,* March 9, 1933; Topeka *Capital,* Feb. 26, 1933.

SOURCES

BOOKS

There are few collections of material specifically relating to Doster. I have gleaned information from a variety of sources widely disparate in their utility. Three helpful reference works were: William E. Connelley, *A Standard History of Kansas and Kansans,* 3 vols. (Chicago: Lewis Publishing Co., 1918); D. W. Wilder, *Annals of Kansas* (Topeka: T. D. Thacher, 1886); and Kirke Mechem (ed.), *Annals of Kansas, 1886–1925,* 2 vols. (Topeka: Kansas State Historical Society, 1954–1956). Mrs. Ben Hill Doster, *The Doster Genealogy* (Richmond: The William Byrd Press, 1945), proved to be a trustworthy source of family information. Two works necessary for arriving at some understanding of Kansas in the late nineteenth century were Paul Wallace Gates, *Fifty Million Acres: Conflicts over Kansas Land Policy, 1854–1890* (Ithaca, N.Y: Cornell University Press, 1954); and James C. Malin, *Winter Wheat in the Golden Belt of Kansas: A Study in Adaptation to Subhumid Geographical Environment* (Lawrence, Kansas: University of Kansas Press, 1944). Some information on Doster was taken from the works of two young scholars, Walter T. K. Nugent, *The Tolerant Populists: Kansas Populism and Nativism* (Chicago: University of Chicago Press, 1963); and Norman Pollack, *The Populist Response to Industrial America: Midwestern Populist Thought* (New York: W. W. Norton & Co., 1966); but I have drawn more heavily from the facts and interpretations in James C. Malin, *A Concern about Humanity: Notes on Reform, 1872–1912, at the National and Kansas Levels of Thought* (Lawrence, Kansas: The Author, 1964); and *Confounded Rot about Napoleon: Reflections upon Science and Technology, Nationalism, World Depression of the Eighteen-Nineties, and Afterwards* (Lawrence, Kansas: The Author, 1961). Annie L. Diggs, *The Story of Jerry Simpson*

(Wichita: Jane Simpson, 1908), contains a statement by Doster on the acceptance of Populist programs during the Progressive era. Good examples of anti-Populist polemicizing are: J. K. Hudson, *Letters to Governor Lewelling* (Topeka: Topeka Capital Co., 1893); and *The Kansas Day Club Addresses, 1892-1901* (Hutchinson, Kansas: W. Y. Morgan, 1901). Some details of Doster's later career were found in William M. Wells, *The Desert's Hidden Wealth* (Los Angeles: The Author, 1934); and Walt Markley, *Builders of Topeka* (Topeka: Capper Printing Co., 1934).

PAMPHLETS

Among the more significant pamphlets consulted was Doster's *The Constitution and the Courts* (Kansas City: Smith-Grieve Typesetting Co., 1910), in which he outlined his objections to judicial review. *William Henry Rossington, In Memoriam* (Topeka: Shawnee County Bar Association, 1908), contains an address by Doster on the legal profession. *The Future Life: Address of Frank Doster, Former Chief Justice Supreme Court, Kansas, before the Unitarian Churches of Topeka and Salina* (Topeka: Crane & Co., n.d.), is a major statement of his religious beliefs. A brief expression of his views on reform is found in a letter printed in Percy Daniels, *Swollen Fortunes and the Problem of the Unemployed* (Carthage, Mo.: Thompson Co., 1908). E. W. Hoch, *The Last War: A Bloodless Battle for Constitutional Government; the Facts, the Law and the Equity* (Topeka: Republican State Headquarters, 1893), is an anti-Populist, anti-Doster Republican tract by the Judge's most important antagonist. Information on the business ventures of Doster and other former Populists was discovered in *An Evening with Senator W. A. Harris of Kansas at a Banquet in His Honor Given at the Albany Hotel, Denver, Colo., on March 26, 1908* (n.p.: n.d.). Irma Doster, *Freedom Has a Happy Ring: A Kansas Bulletin for Kansas Schools* (Topeka: Burge Printing Co., 1960), is devoted in large part to adulation of Doster by his daughter and is of limited reliability. C. S. Burch, *Hand-Book of Marion County* (Chicago: C. S. Burch, 1888) reflects the booming spirit of the eighties. Grand Army of the Republic, Headquarters

Department of Kansas, *General Orders No. 5, Wardell Administration, Series 1932–1933* (Topeka: 1933), gives details of Doster's participation in the GAR.

ARTICLES

"Eleventh Indiana Cavalry in Kansas in 1865," *Kansas Historical Collections,* XV (1919–1922), 524–29, is Doster's straightforward account of his Civil War experiences in the West. His article, "God and the Constitution," *Woodhull and Claflin's Weekly* (April 11, 1874), shows his earliest known association with radical circles. Doster's thoughts on the law, the legal profession, and the courts are given in: "The Relations of Lawyers to Society and to their Clients," *Minutes of the Fourth Annual Session of the Bar Association of Kansas* (1887), pp. 51–58; "An Appeal to the Tavern," *Proceedings of the Twenty-third Annual Meeting of the Bar Association of the State of Kansas* (1906), pp. 179–82; "Legal Phases of Banking," *Proceedings of the Sixteenth Annual Convention of the Kansas Bankers Association* (1903), pp. 118–29; and "Some Bad Decisions," *Kansas City Bar Bulletin* (March, 1925), pp. 4–10. "What Government is For," *The Agora,* II (October, 1892), 120–26, is among the first statements of his political philosophy to reach a state-wide audience. Doster's major outburst against imperialism is "Will the Philippines Pay?," *The Arena,* XXV (May, 1901), 465–70. His denunciations of national prohibition are: "Prohibition Craze," *Plain Talk* (November, 1927), pp. 27–31; and "Kansas Puritanism and Prohibition," *Plain Talk* (July, 1928), pp. 21–27. A rare example of his vitriolic wit is "The College Student and the Old Man Who Wants to Go to War," *The Kansas Knocker: A Journal for Cranks* (July, 1900), pp. 11–15.

S. R. Peters's recollections, "Old Ninth Judicial District: Incidents and Suggestion," *Proceedings of the Twenty-fifth Annual Meeting of the State Bar Association of the State of Kansas* (1908), pp. 143–58, afforded a glimpse into the professional milieu of Doster's first years in Marion County. The story of one phase of the agrarian discontent in central Kansas is told fully in Homer E. Socolofsky, "The Scully Land System in Marion County," *Kansas*

Historical Quarterly, XVIII (November, 1950), 337–75. W. P. Harrington, "The Populist Party in Kansas," *Kansas Historical Collections,* XVI (1923–1925), 403–50, is a sympathetic but useful account by an old "Pop." Other details on the period are in: Powell Moore (ed.), "A Hoosier in Kansas: The Diary of Hiram H. Young, 1886–1895," *Kansas Historical Quarterly,* XIV (May, 1946), 166–212; and Walter T. K. Nugent, "How the Populists Lost in 1894," *Kansas Historical Quarterly,* XXXI (Autumn, 1965), 245–55. The arguments of Doster, G. C. Clemens, E. W. Hoch, and C. S. Gleed over the causes of the "legislative war" are in "The Late Conflict," a symposium printed in *The Agora,* II, (April, 1893), 275–99. Important social questions facing the Kansas Supreme Court during Doster's term are ably discussed in Domenico Gagliardo, "Some Wage Legislation in Kansas," *Kansas Historical Quarterly,* XXV (November, 1939), 348–98. Doster's participation in a sensational case in the 1920's is mentioned in John W. Ripley, "Chronology of Events—Pertinent and Impertinent—of the Jonathan M. Davis Bribery Trials," *Bulletin of the Shawnee County Historical Society* (December, 1965), pp. 54–59.

GOVERNMENT DOCUMENTS

A number of printed state materials were necessary for tracing Doster's public life. The most convenient sources for election statistics were the *Annual Reports* for *1871* and *1872* of the Secretary of State, and the *Sixth, Eighth, Tenth, Thirteenth,* and *Nineteenth Biennial Reports, 1887–1888, 1891–1892, 1895–1896, 1901–1902,* and *1913–1914.* Details of his militia career were in Adjutant General, *Fourth* and *Fifth Biennial Reports* for *1883–1884* and *1885–1886;* material on the Hughes court-martial was in the *Ninth* and *Sixteenth Biennial Reports, 1893–1894, 1907–1908.* The *Third* and *Fourth Annual Reports, 1874* and *1875,* of the Board of Agriculture furnished valuable data on Marion County at the time of Doster's arrival there. The laws which Doster drafted or helped to draft were in the *Session Laws* of 1872, 1907, and 1933; details of their passage were in the *Journals of the House of Representatives* for the same years. For background on the school lands reform law of 1907 I have relied largely on the *Fourteenth Biennial Report, 1903–1904,* of the Attorney General. The *Kansas Reports* for the years 1897 to 1903 contain the opinions of Doster and his colleagues on the state Supreme Court. His activities with the Kansas State Historical Society are documented in its *Eighteenth* and *Nineteenth Biennial Reports, 1910–1912, 1912–1914.* The *Report of the Commission to Revise the General Statutes* (1922) and the *Supplement* of 1923 show Doster's participation in that effort. A federal document, U.S. Senate, 46th Cong., 2d Sess., Senate Report 693, pt. 3 (Washington: 1880) gives his views on the Negro migration to Kansas.

NEWSPAPERS AND PERIODICALS

Because of the scarcity of manuscript material, the newspapers of Kansas were by far the best sources. For his career up to 1896 the *Marion County Record* (Marion *Record* after 1882) was the most useful. The *Cottonwood Valley Times* (Marion), 1887–1889, and its successor, the Marion *Times,* 1890–1893, yielded much information on the period of his rise to prominence in the state. W. A. Morgan's bitter enmity to Doster made his *Chase County Leader,* 1879–1891, an unfailing source of hostile commentary. The *Marion County Anzeiger,* 1887, and the Hillsboro *Anzeiger,* 1891, were important for the Mennonite viewpoint. The recollections of Caroline Doster are in the September 10, 1941, issue of the Marion *Review.* Also helpful for events in this period were: the Florence *Herald,* 1878; *Central Advocate* (Marion), 1891; the *Kansas Commonwealth* (Topeka), 1872; *Kansas Democrat* (Topeka), 1891; *Advocate* (Topeka), 1894; Lincolnville *Star,* 1887; and the Wellington *People's Voice,* 1896.

As Doster's activities shifted to the state level, the leading daily newspapers of the region became the principal sources. The opinions of William Allen White's Emporia *Gazette* and E. W. Howe's Atchison *Daily Champion* could not be ignored. Of greater help for the events between 1896 and 1933, however, were: the Topeka *Capital;* Topeka *State Journal;* Kansas City *Star;* and Kansas City *Times.* Other useful newspapers were: the Kansas City *Journal,*

1900–1902; Topeka *Herald,* 1902; Topeka *Plaindealer,* 1902; and the *University Daily Kansan* (Lawrence), 1931.

Much material was taken from both identified and unidentified items in: *Biographical Clippings,* D, II, III (Kansas State Historical Society); and to a lesser extent, the *Marion County Clippings,* II, *Shawnee County Clippings,* XX (both in the Kansas State Historical Society). The *Scrap Book Containing the Proceedings of the Kansas State Legislature for the Session of 1893, As Published in the Topeka Daily Capital, Prepared for C. S. Gleed* (2 vols.; University of Kansas Library) was convenient for facts and opinions on the "legislative war."

Three periodicals were also consulted: *Proceedings* and *Journal of the State Bar Association of the State of Kansas,* 1886–1933; *Washburn College Catalogues,* 1902–1905; and the *Kansas Historical Collections,* 1900–1925.

UNPUBLISHED THESES AND DISSERTATIONS

Raymond C. Miller, "The Populist Party in Kansas" (Ph.D. dissertation, University of Chicago, 1928), was indispensable for both background and specific information. Two other pertinent studies on developments in which Doster was involved were: Rodney Owen Davis, "The Fencing Problem and the Herd Law in Kansas" (Master's thesis, University of Kansas, 1959); and Joseph W. Snell, "The Stevens County Seat War" (Master's thesis, University of Kansas, 1962).

MANUSCRIPTS

The most beneficial manuscript collection was the Frank Doster papers (in the possession of Caroline Doster Price; Xerox copies in the University of Kansas Library), which consist largely of the typescripts of his speeches of the 1920's. The L. H. Riddle MS diary, 1887–1891 (microfilm copy in the Kansas State Historical Society) presented a close look at conditions in Marion County during an important period in Doster's life. Details of his Civil

War service are in the Alfred F. Doster Military Records (File XC 2656197, National Archives). Stray letters and bits of information were found in the papers of J. L. Bristow, S. N. Wood (both in the Manuscripts Division, Kansas State Historical Society) and Eugene Fitch Ware (University of Kansas Library). The story of Doster's investments in farm lands and town lots is in the A. E. Case collection (University of Kansas Library) and Deed Record Book, 106 (Office of the Marion County Register of Deeds). The Governors' Correspondence (Archives Division, Kansas State Historical Society), contains several letters concerning his efforts to get appointed to the district judgeship. The "Report of the Memorial Committee to the Topeka Bar Association in Tribute to Judge Frank Doster" is among the Thomas F. Doran MSs (Manuscripts Division, Kansas State Historical Society).

INDEX